Christmas
with
Southern Living®
1987

Compiled and Edited by
Nancy Janice Fitzpatrick

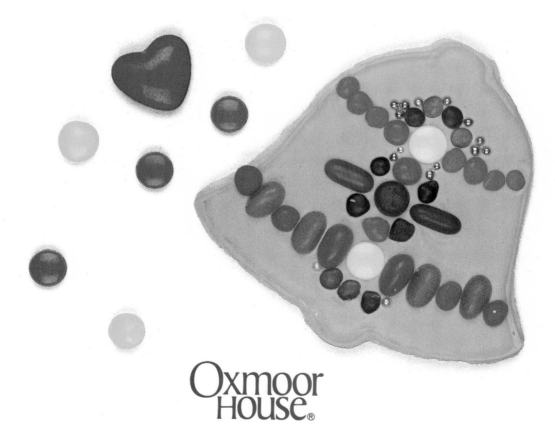

Oxmoor
House®

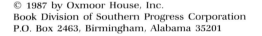

Library of Congress Catalog Card Number: 84-63032
ISBN: 0-8487-0707-9
ISSN: 0747-7791
Manufactured in the United States of America
First Printing

Executive Editor: Candace N. Conard
Production Manager: Jerry Higdon
Associate Production Manager: Rick Litton
Art Director: Bob Nance

Christmas with Southern Living 1987
Senior Editor: Nancy Janice Fitzpatrick
Editor: Kathleen English
Assistant Editor: Alison Nichols
Recipe Development: Kaye Adams, Test Kitchens
  Director, *Southern Living*® magazine
Editorial Assistant: Margaret Allen Northen
Production Assistant: Theresa L. Beste
Artists: Barbara Ball, David Morrison
Copy Chief: Mary Jean Haddin
Designer: Carol Middleton

Introduction 1

Christmas around the South 2

Holiday Traditions 25

Contents

Introduction

We want to help you make the most of the upcoming holidays—to transform your home into a seasonal sensation, to entertain with style, to present perfect gifts. For inspiration, we take you on a photographic journey to festive happenings across the South in December, individually exceptional and collectively diverse, as is this great region. We've also gathered stories of endearing personal traditions that are sure to get you into the spirit of this sentimental season.

To deck your halls, there are beautiful ideas for mantels, centerpieces, entrances, tabletops—decorative splendor all through the house. For decorations, gift ideas, and bazaar items to make yourself, the best designs available are assembled here and accompanied by clear, accurate instructions. Doesn't a progressive dinner (where the group moves from house to house) sound like fun? The menu for this mobile party is included for your holiday entertaining. And over 75 recipes for breads, sweet treats, party fare, and more should help you make every meal a celebration. Some recipes are from readers and some are concocted by our experienced foods staff, but each one has been tested to assure delicious success when you try it in your own kitchen.

We sincerely hope that the ideas, projects, and recipes in this book will enrich your holiday celebrations. We wish you the most fulfilling, happiest Christmas ever.

Christmas around the South

*F*asten your seatbelt. From Maryland to Tennessee to Texas and to Florida, a tour of "Christmas around the South" offers as many ways to toast the town as there are towns to toast. Take Annapolis, Maryland. Colonial heritage doesn't come any richer. Moving inland, we stop at the luxurious Opryland Hotel in Nashville for a rousing Country Christmas. Then it's on to San Antonio where we all remember you-know-what. The Alamo and the San Antonio River sparkle in December. And, toss off your jacket; last stop is the tip of Florida, first for "light" competition (Christmas lights—that is) in Ft. Lauderdale, then on to the Keys where the rhythm slows. In every climate, with every accent, each version is unmistakably Southern.

Yuletide in Annapolis

George Washington slept there. The men who shaped a colonial outpost into a fledgling country strode the streets of Annapolis. Four signers of the Declaration of Independence had ties to the city, and its society before the Revolutionary War was reported to be as fine as any to be found in the colonies. The resonance of that time lingers today, flavoring the experience of being in Annapolis at Christmastime.

At the highest point of Annapolis sits the State House. Built in 1772, it's the oldest capitol building in the country that has been in continuous use. The grassy knoll there is called State Circle, and, following baroque style, streets stretch straight out in every direction, some finding their way to the mouth of the Severn River, where that body of water links Maryland's capital city to the Chesapeake Bay.

The sights of Annapolis are an easy stroll down these streets. A few blocks north of State Circle lies St. John's College, established in 1696. (Francis Scott Key, author of "The Star-Spangled Banner," is among its graduates.) Turn to the east and you'll be at the gates of the United States Naval Academy, founded in 1845. Southeast of the circle is Market Space and the City Dock, the site of tobacco traffic and slave trade in the early days of the city.

Above: In 1694, Francis Nicholson, Maryland's newly appointed governor, moved the colony's capital to the Chesapeake Bay village of Anne Arundel Towne. He renamed it Annapolis after England's Princess Anne and laid out a baroque street plan emanating from the capitol, seen in the distance. Before building was completed, Nicholson became governor of Virginia, where he founded Williamsburg. In spite of that, Annapolis's colonial historic district is, today, the largest in the country.

Right: In attire befitting a proper colonial gentleman, tour guide Rowan Williams holds his lantern high to light the way for visitors enjoying a pub crawl, sponsored by Three Centuries Tours. He stands before the Calvert House, part of which was the home of Charles Calvert, second Provincial Governor of Maryland, in 1727. This property and several other restored buildings in the historic district are now lodgings operated by Historic Inns of Annapolis.

In colonial times, Annapolitans celebrated Christmas in the English style with feasting, churchgoing, and socializing. Today, the narrow streets, with buildings pressed shoulder to shoulder at sidewalk's edge, still bustle with activity. Garlands and ribbons adorn storefronts and facades of homes. Gracious 18th-century historic mansions proffer candlelight tours, greens sales, music, and refreshment. The magnificent Beaux Arts Chapel at the Naval Academy resounds with Handel's *Messiah*, and the clopping of hooves precedes the appearance of a gent in colonial garb guiding a horse-drawn carriage over the cobblestones.

Left: Dapper in their uniforms, two midshipmen pause on the grand staircase in Bancroft Hall at the United States Naval Academy as, in the background, several of their classmates string lights on an enormous Christmas tree. Bancroft Hall, built in the Beaux Arts style popular at the turn of the century, is home to over 4,500 midshipmen preparing for service in the Navy. Today, Bancroft Hall and the other Academy buildings designed by architect Ernest Flagg constitute the most outstanding ensemble of Beaux Arts structures in the country.

Right: The enormous lighted deodar tree in front of Ogle Hall is one of many sentimental traditions in the brimming history of the Naval Academy. Ogle Hall, built in 1739, has served as the visitors' center for the Naval Academy Alumni Association since 1944, and thousands of midshipmen have fondly marked the colorfully lighted tree, visible over quaint rooftops for miles, as a harbinger of Christmas. Early in its long history, Ogle Hall was visited by General Lafayette, who is said to have planted a yew tree in the back yard and remarked that the ballroom was one of the most beautiful in the United States. Governor Samuel Ogle and his son Governor Benjamin Ogle lived there, and other residents have included distinguished citizens associated with public and naval military life.

Among the bundled passersby are glimpsed, here, a young man wearing the uniform of the Continental army, there, a woman dressed as an 18th-century "mollie" (from Molly Pitcher, the Revolutionary War heroine). On certain nights, pass by the Duke of Gloucester Room in the Maryland Inn, and you'll hear a rousing chorus of carols. A peek through the door shows revelers enjoying English trifle and Irish coffee as they pass long-stemmed clay pipes. Wander down to the City Dock, and you'll likely find at least one boat with Christmas lights strung along its lines.

Left: Perhaps the dining room of the Hammond-Harwood House best displays the advanced state of the architect's art attained by William Buckland, its creator. The molding, chimney breast, and mantel rank among his most beautiful work. Here the mantel is embellished with cranberry garlands, apples, magnolia leaves, and fir. To the right of the fireplace is a false door, built there to balance the door on the other side. On the far wall hangs a portrait of Sarah Buckland Callahan, daughter of the architect, painted by the famous artist Charles Willson Peale. She is shown holding her daughter Anne. The painting next to hers is a Peale portrait of her children Polly and Sally. Sally's son, William Harwood, brought these paintings to the house when his wife inherited it from her mother. The Harwoods' Chippendale and Hepplewhite furniture, of Maryland origin, graces the room.

Left: In the quaint kitchen of the Hammond-Harwood House, Christmas visitors stop to sample wassail and cookies served by "mollies," before they move on to the greens sale that raises funds to help maintain the historic home. Area garden clubs supply the materials for the sale and also decorate the rooms of the house in appropriate 18th-century fashion. Brick was recently removed from the fireplace, restoring it to its original state. It was mended with mortar made of limestone and oyster shells, like that used in colonial times.

Above: When William Buckland designed this residence for Mathias Hammond, he placed special emphasis on the parlor, where guests would be received. Elaborate molding circles the room and a finely crafted fireplace stands at the end. Here the room is prepared for holiday visitors, with tea laid ready, and holiday arrangements of cedar, holly, apples, and pinecones. The Chinese export tea service features an intricate "peacock's eye" pattern. A fragrant bowl of potpourri stands next to writing implements on the Baltimore breakfront secretary.

Left: Wreaths of greenery and fruit transform the front door of the Hammond-Harwood House for the holidays. Rich with carved detail, this magnificent door is considered by many to be the finest entryway in the country.

Left: Members of Ferguson's Company, 4th Battalion Royal Artillery, billeted at the Barracks at 43 Pinkney Street, stand guard outside the William Paca House. During the historic district's holiday festivities, the company welcomes visitors to the Barracks, where, properly uniformed, they explain the rigors endured by the troops during the Revolutionary War. Their barracks were actually used by colonial troops passing through Annapolis, though the interior is not the same—the troops often resorted to pulling up floorboards and burning them for warmth. The gnarled mulberry tree in front of the house is approximately 200 years old.

The blur of time in this, the country's largest historic district, casts an added aura of magic on what is already a magical time of year. Part of the blur comes from the fact that these streets are not simply a preserved piece of the past. Many descendants of the early residents call Annapolis home. People live, work, and go to school here, infusing the city with a tangible vitality.

Still, the cobblestones and ships' masts give it a singular, separate charm. And the beauty, the rarity, of Christmas in Annapolis draws visitors from up and down the eastern seaboard.

Left: Each Christmas, the elegant 18th-century William Paca House is decorated with traditional greenery, fruits, and festive foods, and then opened to the public for tours. The dishes displayed in the Paca dining room are typical of those enjoyed by the colonial residents: roast duck, meat pie, chilled oysters, pumpkin pudding, cranberry sauce, Madeira and Burgundy jellies, petit choux (small pastries), dried fruit, and pound cake. The 18th-century Nanking serving dishes are part of a set of chinaware that was probably owned by William Paca, one of Maryland's four signers of the Declaration of Independence and an early governor of the state. In the background hangs a portrait of Henrietta Maria, wife of Charles I of England, for whom Maryland was named.

Right: Undaunted by the snap in the December air, these tourists experience historic Annapolis the way visitors might have two centuries ago—in a horse-drawn carriage. The excursion is a holiday service offered by the Annapolis Hilton. In the background stands Annapolis's State House, the oldest such structure in the country to be in continuous use. Built in 1772, it was in this building that the Continental Congress met for nine months. During that period George Washington resigned his commission as Commander in Chief of the Continental Army, and the Continental Congress ratified the Treaty of Paris, formally ending the Revolutionary War.

Gala Goings-On at the Opryland Hotel

Just driving up to the Opryland Hotel stirs excitement, especially on a December evening when the grounds twinkle with thousands of tiny white lights. Guests can check their cares at the door when they enter this festive atmosphere. A series of events called Country Christmas make a visit here one of the most enjoyable celebrations available to holiday travelers anywhere.

To get guests into the holiday spirit, there's special entertainment including a musical stage show, nightly yule log ceremonies, unique dining experiences, and even storytelling sessions. Elaborate hotel decorations include 110,000 lights (inside and out), 2.2 miles of bright red ribbon, and

1.8 miles of evergreen garland. And guests can wrap up their Christmas shopping at a big crafts, arts, and antiques fair.

At any time of the year, the fine facilities and enthusiastic Southern hospitality at this lovely Williamsburg-style hotel make it much more than just a place to stay. Located about 10 miles northeast of Nashville, Tennessee, the 406-acre Opryland complex includes over 1,000 rooms, a number of fine restaurants, shops, ballrooms, convention facilities, and a vast tropical conservatory. The hotel opened in 1977, offering lodging to Opryland Park visitors. The park, which opened in 1972, provides thrilling rides and lively entertainment from March through

October. There's also the famed Grand Ole Opry, which moved here in 1974 to continue its tradition of delivering the best in country music performances.

At Christmastime, the spacious hotel lobby is a good place to enjoy the decorations, which include a 25-foot-high poinsettia tree and lots of ribbons and greenery. Travel-weary guests can sink into cushy chairs and sofas, unwind by the blazing fireplaces, and indulge in a little people watching.

Each evening at six o'clock in the lobby, the ceremony of the yule log takes place. The entourage, attired in medieval costumes, includes a trumpeter, who leads the procession; servants who pull two carts of logs; a chef, kitchen helper, and high steward; a 16-member choir; a juggling jester; and the seneschal (an official in royal households of the Middle Ages), who reads the blessing from a scroll. Before a log is burned, "over it must be poured wines of the finest vintage," a task to be performed by the high steward. "Next, the chef must anoint it with fat from a huge turkey. Then good serving men shall place upon it, as an emblem of good luck, crossed hairs from the wild boar." The burning of the log is a symbol of the wish for goodwill, health, and happiness for guests and staff.

Judging from the fresh faces and attractive attire, most people stop for the yule log ceremony on their way to dinner. Among the many dining choices within the hotel is international cuisine at the Old Hickory Restaurant (named in Andrew Jackson's honor). Each evening, the chef (a member of the 1988 American team for the International Culinary Olympics) prepares a four-course holiday meal from a different country, in addition to the regular menu. A delicious example of one of the entrees is the Canadian Smoked Goose Breast Hudson Bay (stuffed with wild mushrooms and smoked with maple glaze). Also featured are menus from Switzerland, Austria, Germany, Italy, and France. And there's even a new twist on America's turkey and dressing and pumpkin

Above: The blessing of the yule log is a nightly ceremony in the hotel lobby, invoking goodwill, health, and happiness. This reenactment of a 13th-century English tradition lasts only a few minutes, but in that short time, the holiday spirit fills the room as carols are sung and smiles exchanged.

pie—Tom Turkey Oklahoma (stuffed with dried fruits and finely chopped, highly seasoned meat called forcemeat, and covered with a Zinfandel glaze) and Delta Pecan Timbale with Goo Goo sauce.

For an evening of dining plus entertainment, the *Down Home Country Christmas Musical Celebration* is a real family treat. The hotel's award-winning culinary staff serves a fancy banquet in the 30,000-square-foot Presidential Ballroom. After dinner, the show stars 14 Opryland performers who sing, dance, and act out the holiday story,

Above: The stage show, A Down Home Country Christmas Musical Celebration, *is a heartwarming holiday story spiced with lots of spirited singing and vivacious dancing by Opryland performers.*

Top: At one of the Sunday afternoon storytelling sessions, Jerry Clower reaches for just the right nuance to hold children spellbound.

accompanied by a 12-piece orchestra. The ingenious stage set turns inside out and backwards to create new scenes.

Each Sunday afternoon there are storytelling sessions that are sure to tantalize children's imaginations. Such Grand Ole Opry stars as Tom T. Hall, Riders in the Sky, Archie Campbell, and Jerry Clower narrate spellbinding tales.

For last-minute shoppers, the Country Christmas Craft, Art, and Antique Fair features high-quality handmades, including pottery, jewelry, wooden toys, baskets, quilts, folk art, and fancy foodstuffs; as well as an array of antique country and Victorian collectibles, vintage clothing, and laces.

The conservatory *(at right)* is a tropical garden covering two acres. The glass ceiling is 110 feet high with retractable window shades that help maintain temperatures in the low 70s and a 55-percent humidity. Guests can stroll along meandering walkways overlooking the tropical gardens and sidewalk restaurants, or wander under waterfalls and over streams through the jungle-like foliage. There are lots of inviting spots for relaxing, reading, or conversing. A number of guest rooms have balconies opening onto the conservatory with bird's-eye views of the beautiful scene. During the holidays, conservatory decorations include giant suspended snowflakes and ornaments, mechanically animated figures, and a wall of huge gift-wrapped boxes. At night, music by caroling choirs and musical groups fills this amazing space with magic.

If all these special events aren't enough to keep Opryland visitors busy, arrangements can be made for a three-hour riverboat cruise with dinner and entertainment, a tour of Nashville, a visit to the Grand Ole Opry, or admission to a live broadcast of a Nashville Network television show.

This season will mark only the fourth annual presentation of a Country Christmas by the Opryland Hotel. But the festive experience is prompting many departing guests to inquire, "Can we make reservations now for this time next year?"

A Fiesta by the River

Thousands of multi-colored lights twinkle in the trees bordering the San Antonio River, producing a sight so brilliant, so beautiful, that it outshines the stars. Adding to this celestial splendor is the Fiesta de las Luminarias, in which hundreds of luminarias are placed along the banks of the Paseo del Rio, the River Walk. This vibrant combination of glittering lights marks the beginning of the Christmas season in San Antonio, Texas. Also to be enjoyed are the candlelight masses performed at many of the old Spanish missions, ceremonies to celebrate the importance of animals at that first Christmas, and a reenactment of the Holy Family's search for an inn, known as Las Posadas, which fills the streets with a singing procession of children dressed as angels.

San Antonio, once the capital of the Spanish province of Texas, celebrates holidays with a decidedly Hispanic flavor. By incorporating the Spanish, Mexican, and Indian cultures that settled this area, Christmas here becomes a combination of gaiety and reverence.

Squeals of delight pierce the air at San Antonio's Market Square, as the brightly colored, star-shaped Christmas piñata is broken, spilling its confectionary contents onto the sidewalk. Though excited and enthusiastic in their scramble to collect this holiday bounty, the children are on their best behavior, pending the arrival of Pancho Claus. And what a sight he is to see. Arriving by horse cart, while a mariachi band plays, his brilliant red sombrero sparkles in the midday sun. No passports are needed to enjoy this south-of-the-border celebration. It's all part of the Fiesta Navidenas.

So, throughout San Antonio, piñatas will be broken, animals blessed, and rousing choruses of "Feliz Navidad" sung as this city, rich in history and culture, prepares to celebrate the coming of the Christ child.

Above: One of the most popular customs brought to the Southwest by the Spanish is the piñata party. And it's not as easy as it looks. In some instances`a person is blindfolded before being given a chance to hit the piñata. Often, to add to the challenge, the piñata is raised and lowered while the participant swings wildly at the air. A clay pot containing candy is buried inside the piñata and protected by the many layers of paper.

Above right: At El Mercado (Market Square), an informal piñata-making demonstration is given. Piñatas can be made in all shapes and sizes. Layers upon layers of newspaper and glue form the base of what will be an animal, cartoon character, or religious symbol. Brightly colored crepe paper adds the final touch.

Right: A member of Nuevo Mariachi Infantil Guadalupano, a musical group, performs during the Fiesta Navidenas celebration at Market Square. This group of third-generation performers encourages the crowd to join them in "Silent Night," "Pancho Claus Is Coming to Town," and native folk songs.

Above: Pet owners are encouraged to participate in the Blessing of the Animals ceremony at Market Square. After delivering the general blessing, a local Franciscan priest bestows an individual prayer upon each animal. Inspired by St. Francis of Assisi, this informal ceremony acknowledges the presence of animals at the birth of Christ and celebrates the goodness of God's creations.

Above right: With his brilliant red sombrero, matching poncho, and jet black beard, Pancho Claus is the Hispanic version of our Santa Claus. But only his appearance is different. After Christmas songs and stories, Pancho Claus hands out candy canes and patiently listens to each child's Christmas gift wish.

Right: Dressed in white and carrying a candle to light her way, this young girl is part of Las Posadas, a reenactment of the Holy Family's search for shelter (posada). As the procession moves through the city, the children ask for shelter through song, but are turned away. After reaching the designated shelter, everyone celebrates with a piñata party.

Above: Originally named Mission San Antonio de Valero, this building is better known by another name, the Alamo. Spanish troops posted here chose the name Alamo to honor their home in Mexico and to distinguish themselves from troops occupying a nearby presidio (fort). Surrounded by the modern city of San Antonio, the Alamo remains a monument to the bravery of those who fought for Texas's independence from Mexico.

Opposite: Each December 12, the Mission Espiritu Santo de Zuñiga celebrates the feast day of the Virgin of Guadalupe with a candlelight Mass. Nuns from two local churches sing hymns in the balcony during the Mass. Dedicated in 1777, the Mission Espiritu was one of the last Spanish missions to be built in Texas. Extensively refurbished in 1978, the mission is part of the state park in Goliad and is open daily to visitors.

Florida's Light Fantastic

Temperatures have dropped into the 70s and, for once, there's not a mosquito in sight. Not a very Christmassy picture, is it? But wait. Just as evening falls, a flick of a switch transforms buildings into airy frameworks outlined in light. This is December in south Florida, and the festive outdoor lighting is phenomenal. The number of homes and businesses that are aglow, the quantity of lights used, and the creative applications are remarkable.

There may be several reasons for this inclination to illuminate. The climate discourages the traditional use of natural materials because the heat causes rapid wilting. At the same time, the climate is ideal for hours of stringing outdoor lights—no ice, snow, or sleet to dampen Christmas spirits.

And although the imagery often associated with Christmas—Santa, reindeer, and sleighs; chestnuts roasting on an open fire; and winter wonderlands—is a long way from this semi-tropical region, Floridians love Christmas as much as anyone. It shows in their dazzling light displays.

Above: Yesterday's, a restaurant on the water in Fort Lauderdale, is radiant on all sides. When hungry mariners dock their boats for dinner, they are welcomed with "Season's Greetings" written in lights.

Above left: The first Christmas the owner spent in this house, he had the only show on the street. The following year, his next-door neighbor decided to try his hand at outdoor lighting. Each year, as they both added to their stock of lights, a spirit of competition grew. Last December, as they surveyed the radiance of their properties, it appeared that the first-on-the-block light decorator had won again. Not to be outdone, his neighbor declared, "You've got me beat now, but just wait until tomorrow night." The tree in the foreground (at left), with 550 mini-lights in the star alone, can be attributed to that effort at one-upmanship. Everyone wins in this good-natured competition. These fantasylands have gained word-of-mouth fame that sometimes leads to traffic jams.

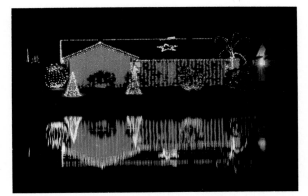

Above: As a star dances on the dark roof, lighted strands stripe the walls of this house. A delineated palm tree and the reflected illumination in the waters of the intracoastal canal succinctly illustrate a Florida Christmas.

23

A Laid-Back Holiday

It could be the beat of a different drum. Or maybe giving the slip to the holiday hustle and bustle. It could simply be that, with a few days off from work, the lure of tropical breezes, spectacular sunsets, fresh seafood, and colorful people is irresistible to some who feel the need to replenish body and soul. Whatever the reasons, quite a number of folks find Key West the ideal spot to spend the holidays.

This 3½- by 1-mile islet, as far south as you can go in the States, is a laid-back place even at Christmas. There aren't a lot of decorations along the narrow, picturesque streets, and you're more likely to hear rocking reggae than a Christmas carol. Though rum is plentiful, eggnog may be hard to come by. But even if the usual signs of the season are not abundant here, goodwill is. There's an easy attitude of acceptance and friendliness that can make a holiday visit to Key West a very merry Christmas.

Above left: One of the colorful characters selling goods at Mallory Square, Mark Freund comes down from Big Pine Key to sell woven-palm wreaths. He also crafts birds, hats, and even Christmas tree ornaments like the one trimming his hat here. Since it's the best place to watch the sun set, Mallory Square becomes a street fair each evening. As the crowds gather, vendors hawk their wares and entertainers perform for donations.

Left: For a gift-wrapped look, the dark green shutters of this Key West house were crisscrossed with red velvet ribbons. Giant bows, brass horns, and pine top the "package." This historic Conch house has weathered a few hurricanes since its construction around 1850. (The term Conch means a native of the Keys, as well as a seashell.) The frame of the house was designed to give a little with high winds.

Holiday Traditions

Without our tributes, Christmas is only a date on the calendar. But often, some simple gesture in honor of this special holiday captures the heart, creating a remembrance to be held forever dear. The wonderful doings on the following pages are of that memory-making kind. There's a grandmother who trims a tree with cherished baby heirlooms of several generations, a family who hold an annual evergreen sale at their homestead gristmill, and a rug-hooking club who meet to complete their last-minute gifts. These stories, and more, reveal the rejoicing Southerner, who lights the season with loving traditions.

Toasts Round a Yuletide Fire

Come, bring with a noise,
My merrie merrie boyes,
The Christmas Log to the firing;
While my good Dame she
Bids ye all be free;
And drink to your hearts desiring.
—Robert Herrick
17th-century English poet

Countless generations have turned their palms toward the radiance of burning yule logs. Each generation has discovered anew the delights of glasses raised high to toast the holiday, the yule log's crackle and glow delivering a rippling backdrop. Such is the stuff of Christmas memories.

The ceremony of the yule log (traditionally invoking goodwill, health, and happiness) is enjoying a resurgence these days, providing a special moment for families to tie into the past and pause in the hectic present.

Whether you've already discovered the pleasures of this ageless tradition or you intend to weave it into your festivities this year, consider the variations shown here. Sharing the log and liqueur preparation with others begins the unfolding of events.

Above: A yule log topped with scented natural materials emits an intoxicating aroma. Simply use melted paraffin to attach cinnamon sticks, dried flowers, and pinecones to a birch or cherry log. Sprinkle pine or spruce oil over the arrangement, top with a generous plaid taffeta bow, and let the log decorate your hearth until the right moment for the lighting. (For more on this custom, see page 13.)

Left: As the scents and glow from the yule log fill the room, pour a round of herbed brandy. Lemon balm, sweet woodruff, sweet cicely, lemon thyme, lemon verbena, or tarragon deliciously intermingle with your favorite spirits.

All you need do to make herbed brandy is loosely fill a widemouthed bottle with one of the herbs, bruising them as you fill, cover them with brandy, and let the mixture steep for a week. Then strain the brandy and, in a decorative bottle, mix two parts brandy to one part each of honey and water. Include a fresh sprig of the herb used for flavoring, and you're ready to relish your yuletide concoction at fireside.

Texas Trimmings

In Texas, state pride runs as deep as the Rio Grande is long. Take the San Antonio home of Mr. and Mrs. Harvey Risien. Beginning with the front door, their loyalties are made quite clear. A grapevine wreath is covered with swirling ribbon in Texas's colors of red, white, and blue, and the lush mass is spangled with Texas Ranger badges. A silvered, weathered cowboy boot is planted beneath the fluffy bow, chili peppers sprout at intervals—and that's just for starters.

In the living room looms a 16-foot noble fir tree (Texans do things big), displaying the same decorative emblems found at the front door. Finally, the Risiens carry their proud theme to the mantel, where the peppers and badges are couched in fir and bathed in candlelight. All in all, it's a lovely tribute to a high-spirited state.

Little Miracles Trim This Tree

Those precious baby things—rattles, spoons, teething rings, milk mugs, even tiny shoes—are forever treasures. But for safekeeping, they usually end up packed away out of sight.

One family has found a way to bring their three generations of baby baubles out of storage at least once a year—they decorate a small tree with them. The reappearance of the priceless keepsakes summons beautiful recollections. Not only do they serve as dear reminders of friends' gifts and well-wishes for the tiny new being, but they revive sweet memories of each family member's infant days. For youngsters, Grandmother's teething ring is a wondrous thing; she was once a wee one, too.

But most important, this sentimental display reminds even the oldest among us of the wonder of our own very personal miracles of birth and life, a fitting reflection as we celebrate the birth of Christ.

The Greens Sale on Big Pipe Creek

In the rolling hills of northern Maryland, Big Pipe Creek gave the Shriver brothers what they were looking for. Andrew and David Shriver saw that this spot, which in 1797 was still wilderness, was ripe for a mill with adjoining farmlands. They bought 400 acres of land along the creek, erected a gristmill and sawmill and a small two-family house, and got to work.

Andrew and David Shriver's venture not only provided a name for their homestead, but also for the community that grew up around it: Union Mills. Their property came to include a tannery, post office, inn, store, and magistrate's office; it was part of a fascinating history.

Washington Irving spent a night at the homestead during a stagecoach journey. James Audubon watched a Baltimore oriole build its nest in a nearby willow tree. This heritage and much more is described in records acknowledged as one of the country's best-documented family histories.

Above: Four generations of Shrivers pose before the gristmill that has been in their family since George Washington's administration. "The interesting thing to me is when you get an event like this started, family members show up from all over," says James Shriver, Jr., shown second from right.

Right: Barbara Steele and Marlene Lufriu of Alloway Gardens and Herb Farm demonstrate ways to make wreaths and other decorations using herbs and dried flowers. In addition to these demonstrations, they also decorate the Union Mills house and offer some of their creations for sale.

Opposite: In 1863, slaves prepared meals in this old kitchen for Confederate and Union soldiers on their way to the battle of Gettysburg, which lies just across the Mason-Dixon line, separating Maryland and Pennsylvania. The kitchen is filled with utensils necessary when cooking was literally a labor of love. In the foreground is a dried-flower and herb wreath fashioned during a demonstration that is part of Union Mills's annual greens sale.

Above: Mrs. James Shriver, Jr., director of the Union Mills Homestead Foundation, is shown here inside the gristmill gathering a bunch of holly, which sells at a rapid clip throughout the greens sale. Behind her are the cogged wheels that connect to the waterwheel outside and turn the large grindstones on the upper level, most of which are original to the mill.

Today, the brothers' descendants keep the heritage alive through the Union Mills Homestead Foundation. The home is now a museum. The restored gristmill grinds flour and corn meal that is sold to tourists and area bakeries. The miller's house contains a gift shop, and the restored bark shed (part of the tannery) is now a blacksmith's shop.

Every year since 1968, the Shrivers have staged a Christmas Greens Sale. Visitors tour the house and enjoy refreshments served in the dining room. Christmas greens fill the various levels of the gristmill, and an herb wreath-making demonstration takes place in the miller's shed.

During the day of the sale, frost often lingers on the banks of Big Pipe Creek. Beside the still waterwheel, ornamented with icicles, several generations of Shrivers carry freshly cut trees and chat with friends and visitors as they sort through piles of magnolia, holly, and fir.

Above: Two young visitors pose with an evergreen wreath chosen to decorate their home for the holidays. Behind them is an antique sleigh that was donated to the Homestead.

This Tree Fills the Bill

For the Carraway family, readying a surprise for their winged friends is as much fun as the bird-watching that follows. Just outside their breakfast room window, they place a small tree on a table and decorate it with edible ornaments for the birds, made from fruit, peanut butter, popcorn, and birdseed. Everyone has a hand in choosing the tree, collecting pinecones, shopping for goodies, popping popcorn, assembling the ornaments, and trimming the tree.

It's a lark to make the bird treats shown here. Bring your feathered friends winging in with pinecones slathered in peanut butter and rolled in birdseed. To make colorful fruit baskets, halve oranges, scoop out some of the fruit, and fill with cranberries and birdseed. Then form a handle by piercing opposite sides of the fruit with an 8-inch length of wire, looping and twisting each end to secure.

There will be cheery chirps when the birds discover the luscious grape wreaths. Simply slide six green grapes onto a 10-inch length of wire and twist ends together to shape a wreath. To make shish kabobs for the birds, spike cranberries on wooden sticks. Even the garland is good to the last peck when you string popcorn and cranberries onto heavy-duty thread.

Jean Carraway (Mom) has a few important tips on bird trees that she has learned from experience. Birds may be featherweights, but swooping landings and fluttering feedings can topple a tree. Assure no downfalls by tying and staking the tree, or weighting the base. Also consider that a flurry of birds may tempt an ambush by cats. Place your tree in an open area so that neighborhood felines can't lie in wait to ruffle a few feathers. Another problem could come from unseasonably warm weather (an occasional concern in Birmingham, Alabama, where the Carraways live). Heat may cause the fruit

to deteriorate, so plan your tree trimming when a spell of cold weather is forecast.

There's one more thing that you should be expecting (and if you've ever had a pet parakeet, you already do). Birds are messy eaters!

Hooking Rugs in the Hill Country

Step across the threshold, and the warmth of fellowship and the creative exchange of craftswomen at work surround you. Today is the Christmas party and monthly meeting of the Hill Country Rug Guild, which is being held at Charlene O'Neil's home in Fredericksburg, Texas. And not once is there a lull in the conversation.

"The purpose of the guild is to freely spread the knowledge of the craft," explains Charlene, "and it is so much fun!" With 15 women seated around Charlene's den table—partially finished works in front of them, baskets of hooks and wool scraps within reach—images of a quilting bee come to mind. But these are modern women carrying on a traditional salvage craft. "As far as we can tell," says Charlene, "this craft is indigenous to the United States."

After admiring each other's most recent creations, and helping themselves to the plentiful selection of Charlene's Christmas goodies, the ladies get to work. This is the first of December and many of the rugs in progress have been promised as Christmas presents. One rug design is an Old English Father Christmas which will be a wall hanging; another design celebrates the recent birth of a grandchild. So hooks are moving at a deadline pace. Shop talk runs the gamut from techniques and designs to jokes about a friend's clothing that would be perfect rug-hooking scrap material. (No member dares to wear clothing of pure wool, lest she become the subject of such conjecture.)

There is as much variety in the colors and patterns of the rugs being hooked as in the women themselves. And though the congeniality of the season inspires gatherings such as this, it appears that it is an interest in crafts that spans differences in ages or backgrounds of the guild members. Charlene explains, "Our art comes out in the interpretation of patterns and colors."

A Legacy of Ornaments

When Joanie and Rand Turner moved to Fredericksburg, Texas, three years ago, they bought one of the city's historic residences, dating from the 1850s. It had been built by some of the town's first German immigrants and at one time had served as a blacksmith's shop and later as a soda water factory. This tie to the pioneer history and culture of the town inspired Joanie's mother, Connie Howell, to make her version of pioneer scrap ornaments. "Ever since we moved into this house, Mother has wanted to do something special for us," explains Joanie, "and this is her gift."

The craft of scrap ornaments in this area evolved from a desire by the German settlers in Texas at that time to have something reminiscent of the splendid decorations found in their homeland. Though materials were scarce, the settlers improvised with scraps of paper and cotton batting. So great was the popularity of these ornaments that by 1870 scrap ornaments were being manufactured commercially.

By adding to the Christmas tree a cranberry and popcorn garland made by her daughter's preschool class, vintage photos of her family, and a few authentic scrap ornaments she has purchased, Joanie carries out a theme from earlier times: beauty through simplicity. And while enjoying this traditional style, which is reflected throughout the house, Joanie commemorates a custom of the pioneers who tamed the land that is now her home.

Right: Although this scrap ornament started out as an angel, through minor alterations by Joanie's mother, it became a Santa. The head is a paper cutout, and the arms and legs are cotton swabs wrapped in cotton. Texas flags and vintage photos also decorate the tree.

Gingerbread Houses and Coconut Snow

Mary Spalten didn't cook the usual Thanksgiving meal this year—unless you consider five gingerbread houses ordinary fare. Beautifully decorated and totally edible, the gingerbread houses look like something out of *Hansel and Gretel*. "It was my mother-in-law's idea," explains Mary, "so we messed up *her* kitchen."

Over the Thanksgiving weekend, Grace Spalten, Mary's mother-in-law, cooked the gingerbread used to construct the houses. Before the gingerbread cooled, it was cut into the various house shapes. After the pieces hardened, everyone helped put them together, using a special mixture of icing and egg whites. *Everyone* includes William, 8, Matthew, 6, and Melissa, 1. "Melissa helped by sleeping during the day," laughs Mary. After the walls and roofs were in place, the children added hard candies to the exterior of the houses and landscaped the yards with foil-wrapped chocolate figures, candy cane trees, and coconut snow—all surrounded by a pretzel fence.

Five houses were made to accommodate Grace Spalten's five sets of grandchildren, and the children got to choose which house they would keep. "We had several requests from boutiques for the houses," says Mary. "But I'm sure the children will eat them."

Above: Mary and Edward Spalten and their children, Matthew, William, and Melissa, pose with two of the five gingerbread houses they made. The brightly colored candies used on the houses complement the colors in the kitchen tile. "Once we got started," says Mary, "it really didn't take that long." But does she mean making the houses or eating them?

Left: A blanket of coconut snow covers the white icing yard of this entirely edible gingerbread house. The gingerbread and icing were made from scratch. Purchased hard candies, candy canes, and chocolate snowmen add color and variety to this monument of sugary delight.

Decorating for the Holidays

Remember how it feels the first time you return home—maybe from shopping, maybe from work—and see your home fully decorated? You know what's there—you pulled it together. But even so, that first time you've been out and then return to see it with fresh eyes—remember that feeling? You notice the way a particular flower sparks a flash of color elsewhere in the room. You enjoy seeing a totally new treatment on a tabletop and a familiar treasure in a place of honor. You feel the season has truly begun, now that your haven is embellished with its holiday best. So much of the season's drama unfolds on the stage you've designed. With those moments in mind, plumb the riches in this chapter as you decorate for Christmas 1987.

Tree Vogue: Topiaries

Regarded as the "art of the tree barber" in the 18th century, topiary gardening is the training of living trees and shrubs into decorative shapes. Topiaries have become popular again, and the trend has inspired designs which explore the use of materials other than live plants. These harmoniously proportioned compositions are being used more and more for holiday arrangements, indoors and out. Additional impact is created by introducing vines, mosses, and flowers into the topiary. The finishing touch is an attractive and sturdy container to hold the formation.

Above right: Common materials produce an uncommon topiary treatment. With a sapling for a base, spheres of grapevines are attached at intervals with florists' pins. Pine, fir, mosses, winter berries, and apples are then placed in the vine spheres. Moss covers the tops of the terra cotta containers.

Opposite: Ivy topiaries sprinkled with tulips, gerbera daisies, ranunculus, lilies, freesia, miniature carnations, and red Christmas balls are placed in silver casserole planters to create this sophisticated arrangement.

A purchased cone-shaped wire form holds two containers of ivy. The ivy in one container has been trained to grow up the form. The other ivy grows down, filling the lower area.

Right: Textures and colors mix to make this corner the focal point of the room. At center is a juniper topiary tree, and spray-painted branches, with gumdrop buds, emerge from either side. A Victorian fishbowl to the right holds a wealth of Christmas candies.

The animal-shaped topiaries, found at the foot of the tree and around the table, are wire frames filled with sphagnum moss rooted with fig vine.

Graced by Angels

Just like mere mortals, angels come in all shapes and sizes. But whatever their form, from pudgy little cherubs to elegant, fair-haired seraphs in flowing robes, they are an integral part of the Christmas story, and they make divine decorations for the holiday season.

On these pages they glide through a dining room, frolic on a banister, and flutter around fireplaces. In every case, they add a sublime elegance, dressing these homes for the holidays.

Left: Graceful handmade Italian angels hover above this lush table setting, suspended from the brass chandelier by supple metallic cording. They are poised as though prepared to serenade the diners who will gather beneath them. Forming a centerpiece here is a grapevine wreath studded with eucalyptus, maidenhair fern, cockscomb, rose hips, pinecones, red berry sumac, canella berries, and pomegranates. Rippling red ribbon repeats the lines of the angels' flowing robes. Separated from the natural materials by a hurricane globe, a single red candle provides festive ambience.

Right: Their demure expressions belie the appearance that these cherubs slid down the curving banister and landed in the mass of greenery on the newel post. One little angel appears to have just escaped a hard fall by catching hold of the diaphanous gold ribbon that weaves around the pine, ivy, and magnolia.

Left: Golden baby angels, wings spread wide and arms full of rosebuds, dangle before this ornate gilt-framed mirror. Made of papier-mâché, they are spray-painted red, then gold, to achieve the right patina. Boxwood topiaries rest at each side of the mirror, their bases wrapped in cream paper that is spritzed with gold paint. More rosebuds bubble along the greenery and nest around the topiaries.

Above: Voices raised on high are vividly suggested in this opulent mantel treatment. An exuberant choir of angels is positioned in the ample garlands that frame the space around the fireplace. The effect is created by generously draping baby's breath-studded greenery to frame a wreath fashioned from dried natural materials. The massing of angels and swirling of delicate ribbon unify the arrangement. Finally, a galaxy of twinkling white lights adds the perfect celestial touch for this heavenly host.

41

The Holiday Glow of Fresh Fruit

Outstanding centerpieces don't have to be exotic. For the striking ones shown here, you can pick up the plentiful materials—apples and oranges, lemons and limes, pomegranates and grapes—in the grocery store. With colorful, voluptuous fruit, the simplest arrangements are extremely effective. And fruit as table decoration is compatible, and appetizing, with all your fancy holiday dishes.

Opposite, a china jardiniere delicately painted with morning glories is the fruitful source for this centerpiece. A flowing garland of shiny red apples, spiked on florists' picks and then wired together, rings the bowl and cascades onto the table. Twining elaeagnus hides the wire. Frothy paper-white narcissus and pink-flushed amaryllis

spring from the center. In the corner, a silver coffee urn boasts a spray of pussy willow, fir, elaeagnus, and magnolia branches. Paperwhites shoot from the heart of the arrangement, and an apple garland curves gracefully downward.

The centerpiece *(below left)* features a row of mirrored place mats overflowing with greenery, ribbons, red and green apples, oranges, lemons, and green and purple grapes.

With handsome accessories, a simple display makes the most of a good thing. In the centerpiece *(below right)*, pomegranates and apples and bits of boxwood and ribbon catch the eye, but the unique accoutrements (an old brass compote and pink marble and bronze candelabras) earn kudos.

Naturals That Last

In some areas of the South, hot sunny winter holidays are a problem when decorating with natural materials. The decorations shown here, created with common Florida flora, are designed to stand up to warm weather. Some tips on their makeup may help with your natural holiday decorations when warm temperatures prevail.

Choose materials that tend to stay fresh, and check water in containers often. Use dried materials, or those that will dry nicely in place. Use more perishable materials as accents only, replacing them as needed. And you don't have to be a natural purist, especially where holiday color and glitter are in order. Add ribbons, beads, or other ornaments to enhance the arrangement.

In addition to hot weather durability, these decorations offer another attractive alternative—a contrast to traditional, or Williamsburg-style, arrangements. They suit contemporary architecture, which is very popular in Florida. So, if your home is modern, these creations may suggest just the flair and form you need for decorating it with naturals.

Left: This tabletop tree has a spiraling golden brown ruffle of bark from a melaleuca tree. The ruffle is filled with a variety of materials, including ornamental poppy fruits, whole artichokes, eucalyptus stems (sprayed gold), and mahogany pods (all dried). There's also fresh Florida holly, Norfolk pine, pyracantha, Australian pine, and oranges. Braided raffia, a gold bead garland, and ribbon are attached beneath the melaleuca bark to repeat the spiral.

This tree shape is a craft foam cone. To cover the cone, sheet moss was attached directly to the shape with craft glue. The bark ruffle was attached with U-shaped florists' pins and reinforced with glue. Other materials were added using wire and picks, or glue. The entire assemblage is nestled in a large brass container.

Left: Over this contemporary fireplace is a wreath lapped with fresh sea grape leaves and encircled by a gold bead garland. Clustered at the top of the wreath are pyracantha and branches of Florida holly. Accents include a single variegated croton leaf, flame-of-the-woods flowers, and dried bird-of-paradise leaves (sprayed gold). Gold balls and brass icicles add sparkle.

The brass hearth bucket holds Florida holly, pyracantha, Australian pine, artichokes, flame-of-the-woods flowers, variegated aralia, and palmetto palm fronds. The palm fronds have been trimmed to shape and gilded with gold spray paint.

Below: Dried and fresh naturals crown whitewashed woven-bamboo door wreaths. Dried materials include the flat leaf circles of sea grape leaves (some sprayed white), diagonal twists of bird-of-paradise leaves, vertical spikes of flax, shelf mushrooms, and whole artichokes. Fresh red-berried Florida holly, Norfolk pine, and Australian pine add vivid reds and greens. Gold balls and artificial fruit complete the center cluster.

To top a wreath in this way, wire a foam cage (available from your florist) to the wreath. Then secure materials to the cage with wire and picks.

Tabletop Medleys

When you are dressing tables for Christmas this year, remember that an arrangement does not have to be complicated or consist of exotic and expensive materials in order to have impact. Single components, when stylishly grouped together, can be simply outstanding.

On the opposite page, extraordinary results are born of ordinary beginnings, as seen in this kaleidoscopic assortment of colors. The elements are glittering pieces of costume jewelry attached to plastic foam trees. Displayed as a grouping, they produce a stunning, 14-karat effect.

An elegant, yet relaxed, mood is established *below*, using elements you probably already have. An oversized brandy snifter is partially filled with cranberries, and nestled in the center is a single red candle.

At right, shells collected during a vacation at the beach are revealed as true jewels from the sea when the unexpected touch of bright-red, mini Christmas balls is added.

46

Mantels Magnificent

Where there's a fireplace, it's usually the focal point of the room. What goes on or above the mantel, therefore, should be very appealing. If you've found the perfect decorations for your year-round mantel arrangement, consider this: for the holidays, leave those accessories right where they are and simply add Christmas trimmings that enhance the existing grouping.

Just a few Christmassy touches can accomplish a holiday makeover. From fancy embellishments (ribbons, ornaments, and balls) to natural materials (flowers, fruit, and cones) some well-placed festive baubles will set the scene for the celebration. And your favorite things will acquire renewed interest alongside the seasonal additions. The examples on these pages illustrate how well this simple approach to Christmas decorating can work.

Above right: This black marble mantel insists on sophisticated treatment. A shimmery wreath is suspended with monofilament from the ornate mirror, which echoes the effect. Iridescent ribbons and balls, silk flowers and plastic berries in peaches and creams, and pale green dried hydrangea are a daring, yet appropriate, mix. Materials are wired to florists' picks and then to a wreath of artificial greenery. More greenery, ribbons, and balls wind around pretty porcelain and candelabras.

Right: After searching for porcelain with the lustrous green wall color in its design, this homeowner unearthed four of the five pieces in the oriental set while shop hopping in England. On a return visit sometime later, she found and purchased the center bowl to complete the set. For the holidays, winterberry and pussy willow branches spring from the urns. Nuts overflow vases and wooden cranberry beads loop around fresh apples and oranges nestled amid magnolia leaves and fir on the carved wooden mantel.

The Festive Whimsy of Folk Art

Perhaps the whimsical nature of folk art touches the child in us. It could be the bright colors, worn here and there from being used and caressed by many hands. It could be the cultures and heritage preserved in beautifully wrought objects. Whatever the reasons, perhaps no accumulation of treasures lends itself so well to Christmas decoration as does a lovingly chosen folk art collection.

Above: Hand-carved wooden passengers on their way to Noah's ark gambol along the swagged fir garland decorating this fireplace. On the mantel, old German Nativity animals graze beside holly. Featured on the three-legged table is a Santa carved by a Wisconsin folk artist.

Opposite: This dining area, off a large open kitchen, is an intimate spot for opening presents Christmas morning. On the antique North Carolina table is a cone of red potatoes surrounded by parsley and topped with a yellow onion—a clever twist on the traditional apple pyramid. Adding to the festive spirit of the room are old and new toys displayed in the Virginia corner cupboard and handmade angels atop the tree and in the greenery.

51

Above: Sleigh bells polka-dot the garland festooning this fireplace, and on the mantel, Santa seems to be swinging his crossed feet as he pauses to check his list twice. Pine and Douglas fir are nestled around Santa, pottery, and the tavern sign, which was painted by a contemporary North Carolina folk artist. The collection of old cast-iron kitchenware below these decorations strikes a nostalgic note.

Left: This free-form grapevine tree becomes a landscape for corn-husk farmers and hand-carved wooden farm animals. In characteristic folk art style, the creatures tilt and swirl around the tree, totally defying the laws of physics. Skirted by a ring of pine and Douglas fir, the tabletop decoration should bring smiles to the faces of adults as well as children.

Right: A popcorn garland and assorted ornaments collected over the years make this tree one almost anyone can relate to. Scherenschnitte (cut paper) ornaments, flags that waved greetings to victorious Union soldiers, and an overshot coverlet doubling as skirt create an effect that folk art enthusiasts can especially appreciate. (For scherenschnitte ornaments you can make, see page 73.)

An Outdoor Welcome

A gracious welcome for guests has always been a dominant theme of Southern hospitality. Perhaps that is why outdoor decorations are so popular at Christmastime. From the moment your home comes into view, visitors feel an immediate greeting and realize that this outward gesture is just a hint of the reception that awaits them inside.

Shown *below right* is an entrance so inviting one can't wait to step inside. The arrangement above the door is based on the traditional Williamsburg door fan. This version is a less formal design, composed of greenery indigenous to the Deep South—magnolia, pine, smilax, and chinaberries.

Pomegranates placed at the top add a dash of red. Blocks of florists' foam covered with wire hold the arrangement and are secured above the door with a nail. Carrying the eye to the left of the house is an oversized fir wreath embellished with a wealth of natural materials.

The simple, yet skillful, arrangement of chinaberries, pinecones, and statice on a noble fir wreath, *below left*, punctuates the arch and echoes the natural wood color of the pine bench beneath it. Should the weather be warm, as it can be this time of year in the South, this would be a nice spot to sit and visit with friends.

Christmas Bazaar

Designed with special friends in mind and inspired by the joy of giving, handcrafted gifts have long been a tradition in the South. Combine your imagination with the collection of ideas here, to create new and lasting remembrances. Stitch elegantly detailed velvet stockings, knit a group of tiny houses to populate a bookshelf, or give herbal bath sets to soothe the mind and body. Your family and friends are sure to appreciate the thoughtfulness wrapped up in every gift that comes straight from the heart.

Holiday Tip: Invest in Gold

If you've priced the luscious metallic and opalescent ribbons available these days, then you know just by looking at these elegant wreaths that they are not particularly inexpensive to make. But with your initial purchase of materials (ribbons, wreath forms, and decorative baubles) and a surprisingly small commitment of time, you can count on enjoying these fancy gilded rings for years to come. By carefully packing the wreaths for storage after the holidays—

stuffing tissue into bow loops to avoid wrinkling, placing the wreaths in oversized boxes, and cushioning them in loose packing material—you will realize a rich annual return on your original investment.

RUFFLED CRESCENT WREATH

Materials:
   14″ Styrofoam wreath form
   25 yards (2½″-wide) gold metallic ribbon
   gold thread
   straight pins
   5 yards (1⅜″-wide) gold metallic ribbon
   florists' wire
   26 yards (⅜″-wide) opalescent ribbon
   26 (1½″-long) gold bead-headed pins
   glue
   6 (12 mm) pearl berry clusters
   2 ounces baby's breath

Wrap the wreath form with 2 yards (2½″-wide) gold ribbon, leaving spaces between ribbon. Secure ribbon ends with straight pins.

Machine stitch to gather 1 long edge of remaining (23 yards) 2½″-wide gold ribbon to make a ruffle. With straight pins, attach ruffle to cover wreath from the ten o'clock to two o'clock positions. Make a bow with the 1⅜″-wide gold ribbon (see Diagram 1). Wire bow to wreath at six o'clock position.

Cut the opalescent ribbon into 1-yard pieces. Gather each ribbon length on a gold bead-headed pin (see Diagram 2). Pin ribbon clusters at random into ruffle and bow.

Glue 4 berry clusters in center of bow. Separate remaining berries and glue individual berries randomly to ruffle. Glue sprays of baby's breath in ruffle and bow.

The Ruffled Crescent Wreath (opposite), the Fluffy Ribbon Wreath (left), and the Golden Grapevine Wreath (following page) are sophisticated holiday accents.

GOLDEN GRAPEVINE WREATH

Materials:
  18" grapevine wreath
  2 silk lilies
  6-ounce can gold spray paint
  5 yards (6"-wide) white tulle
  9½ yards (1"-wide) white/gold
    patterned ribbon
  florists' wire
  12 florists' pins
  glue
  3 (25 mm) gold berry and leaf sprays
  6 (12 mm) pearl berry clusters
  2 ounces baby's breath
  5 (2") gold heart-shaped plastic
    frames

Spray-paint wreath and lilies gold. Let dry. Starting at the five o'clock position on the wreath, loosely loop 2½ yards of tulle in and out of vines around entire wreath. Repeat procedure with 3½ yards of white/gold patterned ribbon.

Make 1 bow from 2½ yards of tulle and 1 bow from 6 yards of white/gold patterned ribbon (see Diagram 1). Attach bows at the five o'clock position on wreath with florists' wire.

Above the bows, attach silk lilies with pins. Glue gold berry and leaf sprays, pearl berries (separated in 2s and 3s), and small bunches of baby's breath randomly around silk flowers (see photo). Wire heart frames into flower and berry grouping.

FLUFFY RIBBON WREATH

Materials:
- **14″ Styrofoam wreath form**
- **13 yards (1⅜″-wide) gold metallic ribbon**
- **135 (1″-long) straight pins**
- **11 yards (2″-wide) opalescent ribbon florists' wire**
- **39 yards (⅛″-wide) gold metallic ribbon**
- **36 (1½″-long) gold bead-headed pins**
- **6 yards (½″-wide) opalescent ribbon**
- **5 (12 mm) gold berry clusters**
- **glue**

Wrap wreath form with 7 yards (1⅜-wide) gold ribbon. Pin ribbon ends to secure.

Cut 11 yards (2″-wide) opalescent ribbon into 6″ pieces. Fold each piece in half lengthwise and from folded end, make 3 cuts to within ½″ of edges (see Diagram 3).

Make a circle with each piece, overlapping ends ½″ (Diagram 4). Pin ribbon circles to cover entire wreath.

Make a bow from 6 yards (1⅜″-wide) gold ribbon (Diagram 1). Wire bow at the eight o'clock position on the wreath.

With 30 yards (⅛″-wide) gold ribbon, make a bow cluster by looping ribbon onto gold bead-headed pins (Diagram 2), and insert at the eight o'clock position on the wreath. *Note:* Do not cut ribbon between clusters. Carry ribbon 2″ to the right, make another bow cluster, and insert with pin into wreath. Continue this procedure around entire wreath form.

From ½″-wide opalescent ribbon, cut 3 (2-yard) pieces, make bow clusters, and insert into big bow. With remaining ⅛″-wide gold ribbon, cut 3 (3-yard) pieces, make bow clusters, and insert into bow. See photo for placement. Glue berry clusters at intervals around wreath.

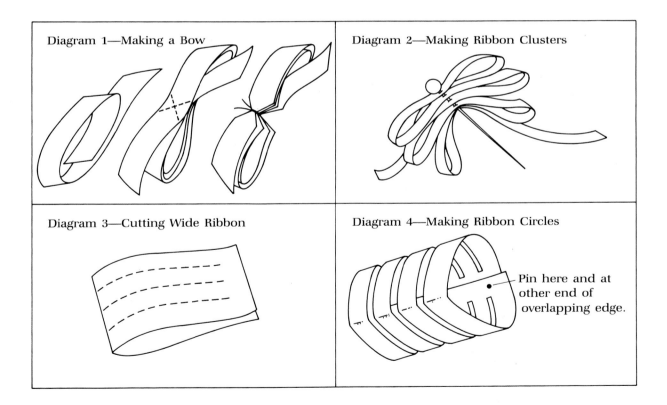

Diagram 1—Making a Bow

Diagram 2—Making Ribbon Clusters

Diagram 3—Cutting Wide Ribbon

Diagram 4—Making Ribbon Circles

Pin here and at other end of overlapping edge.

Sweetly Scented Accessories

Sweeten the seasonal exchange with presents that emit delicious scents. Cinnamon dough formed into little textured hearts imbues a lacy garland and a strictly feminine basket with magical aroma. An heirloom handkerchief cradles colorful potpourri blooms sheathed in illusion net, becoming a pillow to perfume any romantic nook or cranny.

CINNAMON DOUGH: Mix ground cinnamon and applesauce, working it by hand until it becomes claylike in consistency. Sprinkle some cinnamon onto a cutting board, and roll the dough to about 3/16" thickness with a rolling pin.

Place a sheet of plastic wrap over dough, place patterns from page 147 over the plastic, and cut out the hearts with a craft knife. Lift the hearts with a spatula, and place in a cool area to dry, turning often. Drying time is usually around 24 hours, with dough lightening in color as it dries. File any rough edges with an emery board.

CINNAMON BASKET: Make 4 cinnamon hearts as directed. Glue 1" pregathered ecru lace around back edge of each heart. Glue pearl trim around outside edges of the hearts, and use the pattern to cut out 4 pink felt hearts. Glue felt to back of hearts over lace. Tie bows with 1/2"-wide moiré ribbon, and glue to front of hearts.

Referring to the photo, wrap the handle of a market basket with 1/2"-wide ribbon, and glue ends on each side. Glue 2 rows of 1 3/4" pregathered lace around the basket rim, and glue a length of 1/2" ribbon around top edge of basket, concealing edge of lace. Glue 2 hearts to each side of the basket where the handles attach. Fill the basket as you wish. Shown here, a teddy, a lace doily, and a bundle of cinnamon sticks tied with the 1/2" ribbon are tucked into pink tissue.

CINNAMON GARLAND: Make 4 cinnamon hearts as directed. Before dough dries, use a toothpick to make a hole in each, 1/4" from the center top.

With the wooden end of a paintbrush, dot pink paint onto 5 (3"-long) cinnamon sticks. When the paint is dry, cut a 1-yard length of 1/8"-wide moiré ribbon, and thread it through the opening in one of the sticks. Thread on a jingle bell, and alternately thread the other 4 sticks and 3 more jingle bells. Tie a knot in each end of the ribbon to hold sticks in place.

Cut 4 (9") lengths of the ribbon, and thread through the hearts from front to back. Tie a knot near the hole at back. Glue 1/2"-wide pregathered lace around the back edge of each heart. Use pattern to cut 4 hearts from pink felt, and glue them to the backs of the hearts over lace. Tie a heart beneath each jingle bell.

POTPOURRI HANDKERCHIEF PILLOW: Cut a piece of illusion net the same size as a lacy handkerchief or doily with a solid fabric center. Sew net to the inside edge of lace border, leaving an opening for stuffing.

Fill with potpourri made of large colorful flowers, petals, and leaves. (Avoid dusty potpourri because it will sift through the net.) Stitch opening and trim net just outside of stitching.

Ornaments Galore

Simple cutouts in bold colors make graphic decorations, distinctive both in groups and singly. Use scraps of fabric to make a few of these ornaments, or buy yards of red and green fabric and make dozens at once. Fasten them atop packages, inside wreaths, around napkins, within floral arrangements, in a window, or above baby's bed.

And then, of course, you could always hang your extras on the tree.

Materials:
    patterns on pages 140 and 141
    red, green, and white fabric
    thread to match
    stuffing
    red and green satin ribbon in
      various widths
    clear thread
    fabric glue
    pregathered white eyelet lace
    double-sided fusible web fabric

STRIPED STAR ORNAMENTS

Cut strips of red, green, and white fabric as follows: For large star, 2 red (2" x 12"), 3 white (1½" x 12"), 2 red (1½" x 12"), 2 green (1½" x 12"). Cut 1 green 12" square for backing.

For the medium star, cut the following strips: 2 green (2" x 8"), 4 red (1" x 8"), 3 white (1" x 8"), 2 green (1" x 8"). Cut 1 green 8" square for backing.

Using ¼" seams, sew strips in the sequence shown in photo, with 2" strips first and last for both stars. Press seam allowances toward dark strips so that white strips have no shadows.

Transfer patterns to back of striped units so that lines are on a diagonal as shown in photo. Do not cut out; marked lines are stitching lines. Place striped fabric on green

fabric, right sides facing, and machine-stitch, leaving open where marked. Trim seam to ¼", clip angles, and turn right side out. Stuff to a firm, flat shape, and slipstitch closed.

For each star, cut 2 (20"-long) pieces of ribbon. Tack centers to lower left point of star. Let dangle or tie in a bow. Sew clear thread through top point for hanger.

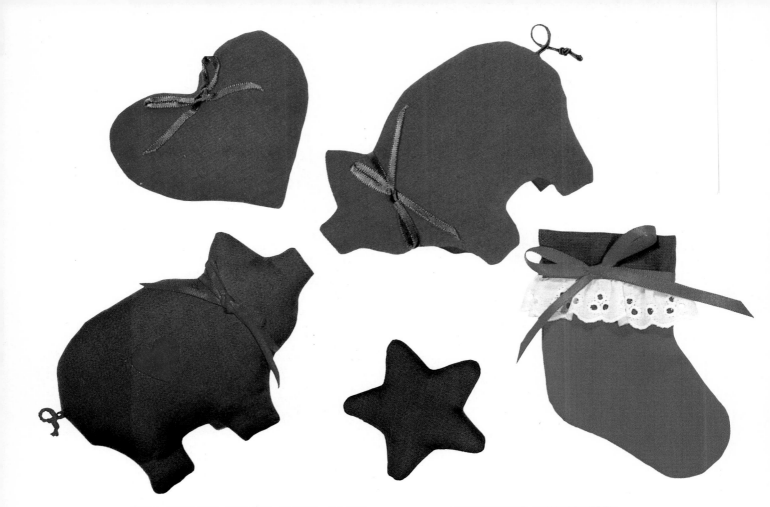

PIG, HEART, SMALL STAR, CANE

For each ornament, fold a piece of fabric in half so that right sides are facing and fabric is at least 1″ larger than pattern on all sides. Transfer pattern to fabric and stitch along marked lines, leaving open where indicated for stuffing.

For the pig, loop a bit of cording for a tail as shown, catching loop with a couple of stitches or a drop of glue, and pin tail between layers prior to stitching.

Trim seam allowance to ¼″, clip curves, and turn. For heart appliqués, cut a small heart from fabric and from double-sided fusible web fabric. Position web on ornament after it has been turned but before it is stuffed, and iron to fuse, following manufacturer's directions.

Stuff ornaments to firm, even thicknesses, and slipstitch closed. Tie ribbon around ornaments as shown, tacking or gluing bow to heart. Loop clear filament through tops for hanging.

STOCKING ORNAMENT

For a red stocking with green cuff, cut pieces of red and of green fabric, each 7½″ x 12″, and fold them in half with short ends together. Transfer pattern to each piece of fabric, and cut out 2 red and 2 green stockings. Place a red and a green piece together, wrong sides facing, fold top 1″ toward red side for cuff, and press. Repeat for other pair, making sure cuffs will align. Place stocking halves together, red sides facing, and stitch. Clip curves, and turn.

Cut a length of eyelet 1″ longer than needed to encircle stocking top. Pin in place so that it overlaps raw edge of stocking cuff by ⅛″, and turn raw ends of eyelet under at back seam. Pin narrow red satin ribbon over raw edge of eyelet, finishing raw ends as for eyelet. Hand-stitch along bottom edge of ribbon through eyelet and cuff. Tie a satin ribbon bow, and tack or glue in place on stocking front. Tack a loop of satin ribbon to back of stocking for hanger.

Sumptuous Stockings: Velvet Adorned

Illuminated by the glistening of gold bells, the radiance of rhinestones, and the lustrous glow of soft, white pearls, these velvet creations lend a luxurious definition to the word *stocking*. The satin lining extends the elegance of this trio right down to its toes.

A diamond pattern is machine-quilted on the front of each stocking, adding depth to the plush velvet and providing a framework for any combination of embellishments. And who knows? Perhaps Santa will fill the stockings with a few sparkles of his own.

For special holiday occasions we often dress ourselves and our children in velvet, so why not our homes? Dress the mantel too, with these velvet stockings embellished with baubles, ribbons, and laces. Velvet began as a woolly, rough-textured cloth called velutto. The introduction of silk and synthetic fibers to its weave produced the sumptuous, irresistible-to-the-touch pile fabric we know today.

Materials (for basic stocking):
   pattern on page 145
   ⅔ yard velvet
   ⅔ yard satin material (for lining)
   ⅓ yard quilt batting
   ⅓ yard muslin
   11″ x 15″ piece of tracing paper
   water-soluble pen
   thread to match

Transfer pattern to velvet, lining material, quilt batting, and muslin. Cut 2 each from velvet and lining material (reversing pattern), and 1 each from batting and muslin. Use water-soluble pen to transfer grid pattern to paper. With muslin piece on the bottom, layer quilt batting, stocking top (right side up) and paper, and tack together. Machine-stitch along grid marks on paper. Tear paper away. To embellish stockings, see individual stocking instructions below.

With right sides facing, pin stocking (in seam allowances only) front to back. Stitch sides and bottom. Clip curves and turn. Fold raw edges at top ¾″ to inside and press. Stitch a 4″ ribbon or cord loop hanger to inside right top corner of stocking.

Pin lining together, right sides facing. Stitch sides and bottom. Slip lining (right sides facing) into stocking. Fold raw edges at top 1″ to inside. Blindstitch to velvet.

PEARL STOCKING

Materials:
   ¼ yard (2¾″-wide) white lace
   ¼ yard (½″-wide) white satin ribbon
   28 (6 mm) pearls
   4″ (¼″-wide) white ribbon (for loop)

Place top edge of lace 2½″ below top raw edge of stocking front and pin. Place the ½″-wide ribbon over top edge of lace and stitch along top and bottom of ribbon. Sew a pearl to the center of each diamond. Stitch stockings together as above.

JINGLE BELL STOCKING

Materials:
   3¼ yards gold and white cording
   ¼ yard (1½″-wide) gold metallic ribbon
   ¼ yard (1¾″-wide) white lace
   23 (9 mm) gold jingle bells
   4 yards (⅛″-wide) gold metallic ribbon (for bows)
   4″ (½″-wide) gold metallic ribbon (for loop)

Cut the gold and white cord into lengths that fit the grid mark lines. Use machine zigzag stitch to attach cord. Place top edge of 1½″-wide ribbon 3″ from top raw edge of stocking. (The top edge of ribbon should meet end of front stitching.) Stitch top and bottom edges of ribbon. Place 1¾″-wide lace over gold ribbon and stitch top and bottom edges. Sew a jingle bell to center of each diamond. Cut 5″ pieces of ⅛″-wide ribbon, tie bows and sew directly above each jingle bell. Stitch stockings together as above.

RHINESTONE FLOWER STOCKING

Materials:
   ¼ yard (¼″-wide) gold trim
   ⅓ yard red, green, gold cord
   gold metallic embroidery thread
   26 (4 mm) red rhinestones
   silicone glue

Place top edge of gold trim 3″ from top raw edge of stocking. (Top edge of trim should meet end of front stitching.) Stitch to stocking. Place multicolored cord directly above trim and blindstitch to stocking. In the center of each diamond, working with 3 strands of gold thread, use a lazy daisy stitch to make 2 petals and a straight stitch for stem. Glue a rhinestone directly above stem (see photograph). Stitch stockings together as above.

A Sweater with Seasonal Style

With the first ho, ho, ho of the year, you'll want to slip on this sweater vest and head for the nearest punch bowl. Knitted in stockinette stitch, the front of the vest features a bold green tree decorated with bobble ornaments and a duplicate-stitched garland.

On the back of the vest, a wreath, embellished with more bobble ornaments and duplicate stitching, hangs over a blazing, brick fireplace. From the mantel hang little stockings, which are actually knitted separately and tacked in place.

The vest has open sides that button at the waist to fit neatly over any top. And with its white background and multicolored design, you'll be surprised at how versatile a wardrobe item it is—even though it must be put away as the ho, ho, ho's fade for the year.

Materials:
  charts on page 148
  knitting worsted (120-yard skeins): 3 skeins white, 1 skein charcoal gray, 2 skeins green, 1 skein red, 1 skein brown, 1 skein light gray
  sizes 4 and 6 knitting needles (or size needed to obtain gauge)
  stitch holders
  Persian yarn in blue, yellow, and purple
  6 (⅝") buttons
  gold metallic thread
  1 skein white angora

Sizes: Directions are for small size (6-8). Changes for medium size (10-12), large size (14-16), and extra-large size (18-20) are in parentheses.
Gauge: 20 sts = 4"; 29 rows = 4" in St st.
Note: Bobble for ornaments is worked in pattern with random colors as shown in photos. With color for ornament, (k front and back of same stitch) twice, (turn work and p these 4 sts, turn work and k them) twice, sl 2nd, 3rd, and 4th sts over first st. When changing colors across row, remember to wrap old yarn over new so that no holes occur.

BACK: With smaller needles and white yarn, cast on 72 (76, 80, 84) sts loosely. Work in k 1, p 1 ribbing for 2½" (18 rows). Change to larger needles.

Row 1: K row. *Row 2:* K first 4 sts, p across, k last 4 sts. *Row 3:* K row. Start chart with 6 rows charcoal gray for hearth except first 4 sts and last 4 sts which are worked in white garter st to form border. *Row 4:* K first 4 sts, p across, k last 4 sts. Repeat Rows 3 and 4 in pattern and follow chart until back measures 20" (20½", 21", 21") from cast-on edge. End with a p row.

SHOULDER SHAPING: *Rows 1 and 2:* Bind off 7 (8, 8, 9) sts at beg of rows. Work across. *Rows 3 and 4:* Bind off 8 (8, 9, 9) sts at beg of rows. Work across. *Rows 5 and 6:* Bind off 8 (9, 9, 10) sts at beg of rows. Work across.

Place remaining 26 (26, 28, 28) sts on holder.

FRONT: With smaller needles and white yarn, cast on 72 (76, 80, 84) sts loosely. *Rows 1 and 2:* Work in k 1, p 1 ribbing. *Row 3:* (Buttonhole) k 1, p 1, k 1, yo, k 2 tog. Work across in ribbing to last 4 sts, k 2 tog, yo, k 1, p 1. Continue in ribbing, working buttonholes on Rows 9 and 15. Work ribbing for 2½" (18 rows). Change to larger needles.

Row 1: K. *Row 2:* K first 4 sts, p across, k last 4 sts. *Row 3:* K. Start chart. Continue with pattern and chart until front measures 17¼" (17¾", 17¾", 18¼") from cast-on edge. End with a p row.

NECK SHAPING: Both sides are worked at the same time using separate yarn. *Row 1:* With first yarn, work in pattern across 29 (31, 32, 34) sts. Drop yarn. Place 14 (14, 16, 16) sts on holder. With second yarn, k remaining sts. *Row 2:* Work in pattern. *Row 3:* Work across to last 2 sts, k 2 tog, drop yarn. With second yarn sl 1, k 1, psso, work across (28, 30, 31, 33 sts each side). Repeat Rows 2 and 3 five more times, then repeat Row 2 one more time.

SHOULDER SHAPING: *Rows 1 and 2:* Bind off 7 (8, 8, 9) sts at beg of rows on armhole side. Work across (16, 17, 18, 19 sts each side). *Rows 3 and 4:* Bind off 8 (8, 9, 9) sts at beg of rows on armhole side. Work across (8, 9, 9, 10 sts each side). *Rows 5 and 6:* Bind off 8 (9, 9, 10) sts at beg of rows. Work across.

FINISHING: Sew shoulder seams. With smaller needles and right side facing, k sts from back st holder; pick up 16 sts along left front edge. K sts from front st holder; pick up 16 sts along right front edge 72 (72, 76, 76) sts. Work in ribbing for 1". Bind off loosely. Add buttons to ribbing on back. With gold thread and duplicate stitch, embroider details as indicated on chart.

SMALL STOCKING PATTERN: With larger needles, cast on 22 sts in desired color. *Rows 1 and 2:* Work in St st. *Rows 3 and 4:* Bind off 1 st at beg of row. Continue in pattern. *Rows 5 and 6:* Bind off 3 sts at beg of row. Continue in pattern. *Rows 7-12:* Continue in pattern. *Rows 13-16:* Join angora yarn and work in pattern. Bind off loosely. Finishing: Fold stocking and sew together on wrong side. Turn. Place on mantel edge and tack to sweater.

Standard Knitting Abbreviations
st(s)—stitch(es)
St st—stockinette stitch (k 1 row, p 1 row)
k—knit
p—purl
sl—slip
tog—together
yo—yarn over
psso—pass slipped stitch over
beg—beginning
( )—repeat instructions in parentheses the number of times indicated after parentheses

Quilt Two Straight from the Heart

As timeless as a favorite old song, quilting never loses its place in our hearts. Maybe that's why big bold hearts seem especially charming on this quilted tree skirt and stocking ensemble. And the appliquéd hearts can be sweetly echoed in your tree ornaments and package toppers.

In the spirit of the season, the tree skirt is a variation of the Star of Bethlehem quilt pattern, popular for over 150 years, and the stocking makes clever use of that pattern's basic shapes. Also known as the Blazing Star, this pattern has always challenged quiltmakers—the pieces must be carefully cut and fitted together for the finished piece to lie flat.

Stitch together this skirt and stocking, and you'll have decorations that will become— like most things quilted—old friends, lovely to unpack year after year.

STOCKING

Materials:
 patterns on pages 144 and 145
 mylar template material
 Note: All fabrics are 45" wide
 ⅔ yard beige with green pindot
 ¼ yard red and green plaid
 ¼ yard red heart print
 ⅓ yard muslin
 ⅓ yard batting
 quilting thread

Make templates from patterns. Follow guide below to cut out fabric.
Cutting guide:
From pindot, cut 4 stockings.
From muslin, cut 2 stockings.
From batting, cut 2 stockings.
From plaid, cut 1 B, 1 C, and 1 D.
From red heart print, cut 1 E and 1 F.

Fold under seam allowances on pieces B through F, and appliqué to stocking front, following Diagram 1. Mark quilting lines 2"

apart on stocking front (excluding appliqués) following the angles of piece B. Mark identical lines on entire stocking back.

For front and back of stocking, baste top, batting, and muslin backing together. Quilt along the marked lines, around both hearts, and around the toe and heel. Trim excess batting away. With right sides facing, stitch front and back pieces together with a ¼" seam. Clip curves and turn.

Make a hanging loop from a scrap of plaid fabric. Pin to outside top of stocking with raw edges together.

With right sides facing, stitch lining together with a ¼" seam, leaving top unstitched and leaving bottom of foot open for turning. Slip lining over stocking, positioning so that top raw edges are aligned and right sides are facing. Stitch top edges together with a ¼" seam. Pull stocking through opening in foot. Slipstitch opening, and tuck lining into stocking.

TREE SKIRT

Materials:
    patterns on pages 144-146
    mylar template material
    Note: **All fabrics are 45″ wide**
    1 yard beige with green pindot
    1¼ yards red and green plaid
    1¼ yards dark green print
    ⅜ yard red heart print #1
    ⅜ yard red heart print #2
    1¼ yards backing
    1¼ yards batting

Make templates from patterns. Follow guide below to cut out fabric.
Cutting guide:
From pindot, cut 1 A and 16 I's.
From red and green plaid, cut 8 B's and 6 yards of 1½" wide bias strips.
From green print, cut 8 strips 4½" x 18" and 8 H's.
From heart print #1, cut 4 E's and 4 G's.
From heart print #2, cut 4 E's and 4 G's.

Turn under the seam allowances on heart E's, and appliqué 1 heart to each piece B. Join 4 piece B's with heart print #1 to alternating sides of the octagon, as shown in Diagram 2.

To each of the remaining piece B's, join 2 H pieces and set in the triangle I's (Diagram 3). Set in units around large octagon. Set in the remaining triangle I's to complete the center unit.

Center border strips on each side and stitch in place, mitering corners. Appliqué small hearts over border seams, alternating prints.

Cut backing and batting pieces slightly larger than pieced top. Baste top, batting, and backing together. Using red thread, baste a line from the center point of circle to outer edge (radius), bisecting 1 piece H. This will be the cutting line.

Trace the heart G template in center of each border. Mark a 1½" grid through border strips and beige pindot triangles next to them, as for stocking, not marking through heart outline. Mark quilting on central section A as shown on pattern. Quilt along marked lines, around hearts, and around plaid pieces, being careful not to cross the red thread line.

Cut along the red line. Finish all raw edges with bias binding.

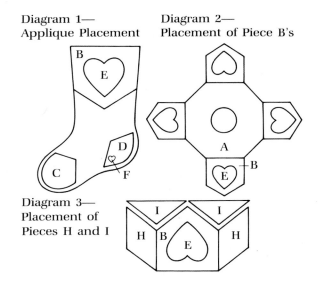

Diagram 1—
Applique Placement

Diagram 2—
Placement of Piece B's

Diagram 3—
Placement of
Pieces H and I

Lacy Ornaments from Plain Paper

As delicate as a butterfly's wing and as intricate as a bit of old lace, papercutting, also known by the German word *scherenschnitte*, is an art that has been popular all over the world for hundreds of years.

Designs can range from simple to ornate and can be used as gift-wrap embellishments or tree trimmings. Any lightweight paper, such as the antique-look parchment paper shown here, can be used. But gold, silver, and colored papers can put a gleam in your decorations.

Transfer the patterns on page 151 to parchment paper. Using a small pair of very sharp-pointed scissors or a small craft knife with a swivel head, cut out the smallest openings on the design first, and work from the inside out. For smoother cutting, hold the scissors stable and feed the paper into the scissors.

A Herd of Holiday Reindeer

Make a handsome herd of reindeer to roam across your mantel, or make just a few to tuck away in a wreath or windowsill. Crafted from scraps of wood and twigs to which the bark is still attached, each reindeer is whimsically unique down to its long, knobby twig legs.

The reindeer have 5 pieces: legs, body, neck, head, antlers. Because each reindeer is made from limbs and twigs, there are no specific measurements for the pieces.

For the legs, choose 4 twigs of approximately the same diameter and trim them to the same length. Drill two ¼"- to ½"-wide holes (depending on size of legs) ¼" to ½" deep on each side of the body. (See photograph.) Add a drop of wood glue to each hole and insert legs. Let dry. (It may be necessary to whittle down the tops of the legs for them to fit in holes.)

For head, measure ¼" to ⅝" from one top edge of the body, and drill a hole same size as for legs. Insert a 1"-long twig, (same diameter as legs) for the neck. On underside of head, drill a hole of the same diameter. Use a nail to make 2 small holes in the back portion of the top of head. (Antlers will be inserted here.) Place head on neck.

For antlers, use 2 small twigs of about the same height. Dot a bit of wood glue on ends of antlers and insert into holes in head. Finish with a red bow around the neck.

Old-Time Santa

This version of the kind old gentleman looks like an aged treasure from the flea market. But it's really an application of a mineral spirits and oil mixture to painted wood that gives Santa his antique appearance.

The rounded ends of the two-inch wood piece exaggerate Santa's "bowl full of jelly" belly, while his mittened hands seem to be patting this celebrated feature.

Materials:
> patterns on pages 142 and 143
> 13" x 14" piece of 2" wood
> band saw or jigsaw
> sandpaper
> wood sealer
> gesso
> paintbrushes
> acrylic paints (dark red, medium flesh, black, white, manganese blue, metallic gold, dark green)
> transparent acrylic gel medium
> burnt umber oil
> mineral spirits
> 0000 steel wool
> varnish

Transfer pattern to wood and cut out. Trim a 2¼"-long flat base on bottom curved side to stabilize Santa. Sand all sides and seal. Paint wood with one coat of gesso. Let dry and sand. Paint entire surface with 2 coats of red paint.

Transfer painting details to front of piece. For back of piece, transfer hat, hair, hatband, pom-pom, and belt. For beard, hatband, and cap pom-pom, mix half white paint and half gel medium and apply. Let dry overnight. Paint cheeks and nose with a watered down mixture of medium flesh and red. Paint eyes with black paint and let dry. Highlight eyes with a small white dot on either side of each eye. The belt is black with a gold buckle. For mittens, mix manganese blue, white and a bit of red. Leaves on mittens are dark green; flowers are white dots with gold centers.

Antique piece by applying a mixture of burnt umber oil and mineral spirits to the wood. When dry, use steel wool to highlight the piece by rubbing off oil and mineral spirits in certain areas. Wipe off piece and finish with 2-3 coats of varnish.

Greetings of Joy

Ring in the season with this vivacious message of welcome. There will be absolutely no question about the warmth of hospitality in a home where this greeting hangs.

Ribbons and holly cut from contrasting fabrics are appliquéd to frame the machine-embroidered message. Tiny French knots scattered across the front repeat the pindot design of the fabric and subtle quilting emphasizes the appliqué. A yellow bell, nestled between the holly and ribbon, decorates the top and adds a splash of brightness to the joyous proclamation.

Materials:
- patterns on pages 152 and 153
- ⅔ yard light-colored print fabric (for front and back)
- scraps of red, green, and yellow fabric (for ribbon, bow, holly and bell)
- craft glue
- tear-away backing for appliqué
- thread to match
- red embroidery floss
- 1¼ yards red piping
- ⅓ yard batting
- white thread (for quilting)
- quilting needle

Transfer pattern for front and back to light-colored fabric and cut out. Transfer remaining patterns to fabrics and cut out. Glue ribbon, bow, bell, and holly to front piece, as shown in photograph.

Transfer embroidery details and words to front piece. Cut a piece of tear-away backing same size as front piece, and pin it to back of fabric. Using 1 strand of embroidery floss and a machine satin stitch, embroider words and appliqué designs. Remove backing and trim threads.

Cut a 42" length of piping. Pull fabric covering back 1" on either end to expose cord. Trim cord to exact length needed, and wrap ends in tape to prevent raveling. Fold excess fabric under even with cord, and restitch fabric to piping. With folded edge of piping towards center, stitch piping to right side of front piece. Hand-stitch the finished piping ends together.

Using back piece as a pattern, cut out a piece of batting. Place back piece on front piece, right sides facing, with batting on top and piping inside. Leaving an opening for turning, and following previous stitch line, stitch all layers together. Turn and close opening. Hand-quilt around the perimeter of sign and around ribbon design. Using 1 strand of embroidery floss and following pattern, embroider French knots. Using 1 strand of green thread, embroider the clapper of the bell.

Cross-Stitch a Memory

Christmas carols help, and shopping for gifts is a boost, but Christmas really becomes a celebration when you get home with family and friends. Perhaps that is why the heart-shaped frame fits so well around this cross-stitch piece, much like the arms that welcome you home.

But even if you can't get home for the festivities, this stitchery, with its garland of popcorn and cranberries, may remind you of good times you had helping the family prepare for Christmas, and prompt you to begin traditions of your own.

Materials:
   chart and color key on page 143
   14-count (14″ x 10″) green Aida cloth
   #24 tapestry needle
   embroidery floss (see color key)
   purchased heart-shaped frame

Work design on Aida cloth according to chart, using 2 strands of floss for cross-stitching and backstitching. Trim design to fit frame, mount, and place in frame. If purchased frame has no backing, block design on cardboard before placing in frame.

These Goodie Bags Are a Cinch

With quick and simple machine work, you can probably whip out one of the food gift packages shown here while the goodies bake. The bags and covered basket are appliquéd with simple shapes, and the words are machine-embroidered.

"CHRISTMAS BREAD" BAG

Materials:
    patterns on page 150
    ⅓ yard light-colored fabric (bag)
    fabric scraps (tan, white, and green)
    glue stick
    water-soluble marking pen
    6" x 8" piece of tear-away backing
    red embroidery floss (holly berries)
    matching threads
    tissue paper
    ribbon or cord

Note: Bag holds single loaf of bread.

For bag, cut out 2 (9" x 17") pieces from light-colored fabric. Use patterns to cut bread shapes and leaves. Glue bread slice to loaf as pattern indicates. Glue loaf and leaves to bag, and transfer the words *Christmas Bread* (see photo). Draw ³⁄₁₆" circles for berries with the water-soluble marking pen.

Pin tear-away backing behind design. Embroider red berries. With matching threads and a machine satin stitch, stitch lines on bread loaf, around leaves, and for words. Remove backing and clip threads.

Stitch bag front to back, right sides facing and leaving 1 end open, with a ¼" seam. In stitching short edge, round corners. Trim seam; clip at corners. Turn bag right side out. Fold end under ¼" and ¼" again; press. Topstitch around opening to hem.

Wrap bread loaf in foil or plastic wrap, and stuff tissue paper into bag to cushion loaf. Tie bag closed with ribbon or cord.

"FROM MY KITCHEN" BASKET COVER

Materials:
   patterns on page 150
   ¼ yard red print fabric (cover)
   scrap of white fabric (center circle)
   fabric scraps (brown and red)
   glue stick
   5″ square of tear-away backing
   embroidery thread (brown and red)
   ½ yard (½″-wide) lace
   1 yard (⅛″-wide) ribbon
   scrap batting
   7″-diameter basket with handle

Note: Patterns are for a 7″-diameter basket with handles. Adjust patterns for other baskets by measuring diameter and checking handle placement.

Cut out cover, center circle, hearts, and gingerbread man from patterns. (If dark fabric can be seen through white fabric, cut 2 white center circles for a double thickness.) Transfer words *From My Kitchen* and glue gingerbread man and hearts on white circle (see photo). Pin tear-away backing behind design. Make French knot brown eyes and red buttons on gingerbread man, and backstitch red mouth. With a machine satin stitch and matching threads, appliqué the gingerbread man and hearts, and embroider the words. Remove backing and clip threads.

Machine-appliqué white circle to center of front cover. With raw edges together, pin lace around front cover, cutting and folding lace ends under on either side of basket handles; then stitch. Cut ribbon in 9″ lengths. On either side of handles, pin a ribbon, aligning end with raw edge of fabric. (Pin loose ribbon ends at center of cover to avoid catching them in seam when sewing cover front and back together.)

Stitch cover back to front, including around handle indentations, with right sides facing and lace and ribbon to the inside. Leave a 2½″ opening for turning (away from handle areas). Clip curves to avoid puckering, especially at the handle indentations. Turn cover right side out.

Use cover as a pattern to cut a circle from batting. Slip batting inside cover; then stitch opening closed. Quilt around center circle, gingerbread man, and hearts. Place cover on basket, tying ribbons together around handle. Trim ribbons to desired length.

"COOKIES" BAG

Materials:
   patterns on page 151
   ⅓ yard light-colored fabric (bag)
   fabric scraps (yellow and tan)
   glue stick
   5″ x 8″ piece of tear-away backing
   matching threads
   embroidery floss (red and green)
   1¼ yards (¾″-wide) ribbon

From light-colored fabric, cut out 2 (11″) squares for bag and 2 (1½″ x 11½″) strips for casing. Use patterns to cut out cookies.

Transfer the word *Cookies* to bag front, 1½″ from center bottom, and glue cookies over word (see photo). Pin tear-away backing behind design. With machine-satin stitch and matching threads, stitch around cookies and embroider word. Embroider chips on "chocolate" cookies.

Stitch bag front to back, right sides facing, with a ¼″ seam. Round corners at bag bottom. Trim seam, clipping at corners. Turn bag right side out. Fold open end under ¼″ and ¼″ again; press and topstitch. Press top, bottom, and ends of casing pieces under ¼″. Pin 1 casing piece on bag front, 1″ from top edge. Topstitch top and bottom casing edges (leave ends open for ribbon). Repeat procedure for back casing. Cut ribbon in half. Pin a safety pin to ribbon ends to feed through casings; remove pin.

Fill bag with cookies wrapped in foil or plastic wrap. Draw ribbons tight and tie into decorative bows.

Photo Finish: Holly Leaves and Berries

A child on Santa's knee, relatives from afar, the family round the tree—such precious images captured on film deserve a fitting and festive presentation. Frame those memorable moments in a dimensional photo mat like the one shown here. Holly leaves and berries, fashioned from paper, flourish in a colorful border. And this easy embellishment can also be applied to gift wraps or cards.

HOLLY MAT

Materials:
- **pattern on page 151**
- **red mat board**
- **heavy textured watercolor paper**
- **craft knife and sharp blades**
- **single-hole punch**
- **craft glue**
- **green construction paper**
- **frame with a ½" rabbet (recess on back of frame)**
- **glass and corrugated cardboard to fit frame**
- **masking tape**

Depending on the size of the photo that you wish to frame, you can buy a precut mat, have your local framing shop prepare one, or cut it yourself. (Sample dimensions for a 5" x 7" photo mat: outer dimensions—8" x 10", opening dimensions—4½" x 6½".)

Cut watercolor paper to match outside dimensions of mat (8" x 10"). Cut inside opening of watercolor paper mat slightly larger than red mat board opening (4¾" x 6¾"), allowing a ⅛" red border to show. For holly berries, punch holes in watercolor paper with single-hole punch to make tiny red circles. Group red circles in clusters. Glue paper mat to mat board.

Transfer leaf patterns to green paper and cut out. Lightly score spine of leaf, and fold or pinch along this line to give leaf dimension. Apply a thin line of glue along leaf spines, and position groups of leaves around red berries (tiny circles).

To avoid crushing leaves under glass, cut ¼" strips of mat board, 2 the length of the mat, and 2 the width of the mat. Insert glass in frame; then glue strips to inside of frame, just behind glass. Insert mat in frame, resting on strips. Tape photo in place behind mat. Insert cardboard backing and secure with masking tape.

Checkers Anyone?

Checkers is a game to be enjoyed by all ages, and this gingham dog and calico cat gameboard will entice young and older players alike.

The antiqued look is achieved by sanding the wood after paint and stain have been applied. Wooden dowels on each side of the board will keep all the pieces together for many hours of good old-fashioned fun.

Materials:
   pattern on pages 138 and 139
   16″ (1 x 12) pine shelving
   band saw or jigsaw
   10″ (⅞″-wide) dowel (for checkers)
   drill with ¼″ bit
   acrylic paints (white, black, green, pink, yellow, red, brown, blue)
   paintbrushes
   fine sandpaper
   cherry wood stain
   2 (¼″ x 6″) dowels (for stands)
   wood glue

Transfer pattern to pine shelving and cut out. To make checkers, cut ⅞″-wide dowel into 32 (¼″) pieces. Drill a hole through center of each checker. Drill ½″-deep holes for the 2 dowel checker stands as indicated on pattern.

Transfer painting details to board and paint. (Do not seal wood first.) Paint 16 checkers red and 16 black. Let dry.

For an antiqued look, lightly sand surface of board and checkers. Sand more heavily along the edges. This will remove some paint to reveal wood beneath. Apply wood stain to board and ¼″-wide dowel. Wipe off as much stain as desired to achieve the antiqued effect. Let dry.

Put a drop of glue in each checker stand hole and insert stained dowels. Let dry. Slide checkers onto dowels.

Knit a Festive Neighborhood

A whimsical neighborhood is no farther away than your knitting bag full of scrap yarn. These diminutive domiciles are worked in the round on double-pointed needles, and then embellished with embroidered details such as finely wrought wreaths, French knot doorknobs, and outline-stitched door and window facings.

Simply change the needle size to knit a larger house, and add another few rows to construct a two-story dwelling. Then arrange the little houses in a favorite spot or loop clear cord through the back to hang them from the tree.

Materials:
 charts on page 147
 scraps of sportweight yarn (for
  houses and embroidered details)
 4 double-pointed needles per
  ornament
 stuffing

Note: Houses are worked in St st. Size variations come from using sizes 1 through 6 needles. When changing colors across row, remember to wrap old yarn over new so that no holes occur.

Cast 36 sts onto 3 needles, 12 sts per needle. *Rows 1 and 2:* Connect and knit in the round. Work even in St st. *Rows 3-7:* Work design from chart, knitting door and windows as indicated. *Rows 8 and 9:* Work even in main color.

For a 2-story house, use top floor chart for front, and work 5 more rows. Add windows on sides and back if desired.

Follow chart for gables and dec 1 st each edge on k rows. Attach more yarn to work second gable.

Attach main color yarn to back of house (see chart) and bind off 12 sts.

The 12 sts on the front are knit up for roof. Attach yarn in roof color and inc 1 st each

edge (14 sts). Work even until roof reaches gable top. End with a p row.

Next row: K 8 sts, bind off 2 sts, k rest of row (makes opening for chimney). P back, casting on the 7th and 8th sts. Work even until roof fits gables. Bind off and leave a length of yarn. Sew roof onto the back of the house. Sew gables onto the roof, sewing from the peak down each side.

CHIMNEY: Cast on 3 sts in chimney color, work even for 1½", and bind off. Fold chimney piece in half, short ends together, and sew down 1 long side. Insert fluffed gray yarn for smoke. Sew the other side and tack in place.

Embroider details as desired. Shape by dampening slightly and squaring the corners. Fill with stuffing.

Standard Knitting Abbreviations

St st—stockinette stitch (k 1 row, p 1 row)
st(s)—stitch(es)
dec—decrease
k—knit
inc—increase
p—purl
"Work even" means to work in pattern stitch with no increases or decreases.

Herbal Bath Gifts

They're crisp and refreshing as only nature can be—these after-shaves and body rubs infused with herbs. Mix up a batch of after-shaves to pamper that special man on your list and an array of body rubs for your active friends; then present your tinctures in clearly beautiful bottles.

Witch hazel, itself derived from the leaves and bark of the witch hazel shrub, becomes the soothing base for these lotions. Measures of citrus and herbs lend zest to after-shaves. And all manner of herbs season body rubs, creating concoctions to soothe muscles that have taken down the tree or exercised away holiday plum pudding.

HERBAL AFTER-SHAVES: Place ½ cup of bruised, fresh and dried herbs in a measuring bowl, and cover with boiling water to 1-cup mark. Cool and strain into 1½ cups witch hazel. Label "For External Use Only."

For a Citrus Woods after-shave, use rosemary sprigs (half fresh, half dried), and add 6 drops of orange oil to the mixture after it is blended with witch hazel. Caribbean Bay after-shave is spiced with lemon verbena sprigs (half fresh, half dried), 4 bruised fresh bay leaves, 2 dried bay leaves, and 1 teaspoon grated lemon peel.

HERBAL BODY RUBS: Loosely fill a wide-mouthed jar with fresh, bruised herbs. Cover with witch hazel, seal, and steep for 2 weeks, or until scented. For more fragrance, use strained infusion to cover another batch of herbs, or add 6 drops of essential oil to each 2 cups of mixture. Strain, bottle, and label "For External Use Only."

Make Myrtle and Lavender body rub by steeping myrtle and lavender leaves and flowers, if available, in witch hazel. Use lavender oil if you want to strengthen the scent. For a Mixed Herb body rub, try sprigs of sage, thyme, sweet marjoram, wintergreen, and calendula petals. Other herbs to try are savory, wormwood, rosemary, and lemon balm. A fresh sprig adds a decorative look to the final concoction.

Stencil a Thicket of Trees

A misty thicket of trees marks the perimeter of this muslin table runner, and a small copse of trees adorns a muslin bottle bag. Subtlety is definitely the effect, owing to minimal stenciling combined with the warmth of quilting.

On the table runner, trios of stenciled and quilted trees alternate with trios of outline-quilted trees. The same stencil used for the runner transforms a simple bottle bag into a coordinated table accessory. Stitch up several as gift wraps, arrange them on a buffet, and your presents will help decorate until they pass into the hands of friends.

STENCILED AND QUILTED TREE RUNNER

Materials:
   pattern on page 149
   stencil plastic or heavy plastic (14-16 mil)
   permanent black marker
   craft knife
   1½ yards (44"-wide) unbleached muslin
   washable or vanishing fabric marker
   green stencil paint
   stencil brush or stencil sponge
   1½ yards quilt batting
   quilting thread
   spray fabric protector (optional)

Cut 2 (7") squares of plastic for the stencils and 2 (6") squares of plastic for the quilting templates.

With black marker, mark the center points of both 7" squares. Transfer the tree pattern to one of the squares, leaving 1" around the design and drawing the large tree with solid lines and the small trees with broken lines. This will be stencil #1. On the other square, transfer small trees with solid lines and

large tree with broken lines. This will be stencil #2. With a craft knife, cut out along solid lines; broken lines will be used for reference to position stencils. Repeat above procedure with the 6" squares of plastic to make quilting templates.

Wash and iron muslin. Cut a piece 19" x 49". With fabric marker, mark muslin ½" from edge on all four sides. Mark center points on each side. Position stencil #1 on the ½" line, aligning center points on stencil and fabric. Load brush and work paint down to a light consistency on newspaper. Using an up-and-down stippling motion, paint large tree lightly. Place stencil #2 over stenciled tree, lining it up with broken outline on stencil. Stencil small trees darker, as shown in photo. Wash brush often as you work to keep drying paint from hardening in bristles.

To mark quilted-only trees between stenciled trees, place quilting template of large tree beside stenciled design along ½" line so that broken lines of a small tree are almost touching a just-painted small tree. Transfer big tree pattern, and repeat with quilting template of small trees. Continue alternating stenciled trees with trees to be quilted, beginning at the center point for each edge of runner top. When finished, heat-set design, following paint manufacturer's directions. With quilt template, mark large tree outline on stenciled small trees.

Working outward from center of piece, lightly draw a 2" grid. Do not draw on trees.

Cut a piece of muslin and a piece of batting 2" larger than the top. Layer stenciled top, batting, and backing and baste together securely. Quilt on marked grid, around all stenciled trees, and around outlined trees. Trim away excess batting and backing.

From leftover muslin, make 1¾" binding strip, 4½ yards long. With right sides facing, stitch strip to front of quilted piece, mitering corners. Fold over to back. Turn raw edge under and slipstitch binding to backing. If desired, spray runner with fabric protector, following manufacturer's directions.

STENCILED BOTTLE BAG

Materials:
  8″ x 20″ piece of unbleached muslin
  thread to match muslin
  stencils from tree runner
  green stencil paint
  16″ (1½″-wide) ruffled eyelet lace with
    grosgrain ribbon insert
  red tissue
  20″ (1″-wide) red satin ribbon

Wash and iron muslin. Centering stencils on each half of bag with tops of trees toward short edges, stencil trees as for runner. Fold in half with short ends together and right sides facing. Stitch sides with a ¼″ seam, and turn.

Fold raw edges to inside ¼″ twice and stitch. Stitch lace around top edge, folding under and overlapping ends at one side seam. Fill bag with tissue, as shown here, and cinch around bottle with red ribbon.

Poinsettias in Versatile Needlepoint

Known in its native Mexico as the fire flower, the blazing red poinsettia is one of the most recognizable of the Christmas plants. Named after Dr. Poinsett, who brought the plant to the United States, the poinsettia, with its vivid red and green colors, is a natural for holiday decorating.

Worked from one chart, the needlepoint belt or card holder—or both—will make a lovely hostess gift.

POINSETTIA BELT

Materials:
    charts and color key on page 147
    stitch diagrams on page 147
    6″ x 4″ piece of #10 mesh plastic canvas
    #20 tapestry needle
    embroidery floss: 1 skein each of gold, light green, dark green, dark red; 2 skeins each of light red, medium red, black (see color chart)
    6″ x 45″ piece of black cotton fabric
    3″ x 45″ piece of quilt batting
    black thread
    2″ (¾″-wide) length of black Velcro

Note: Buckle design is worked in a continental stitch, using 2 strands of floss. All outlines are backstitched, using a single strand of black floss.

Mark belt slots on canvas and cut out the openings. Work design on canvas according to chart. Work edges of slots in black also. Finish outer edge of buckle, using an overcast stitch and a double length (12 strands) of black floss. Take 2-3 stitches in corners for best coverage.

To make the belt, add 5″ to the waist measurement. Cut the black fabric and the batting to this length. Fold black fabric in half lengthwise with right sides facing, and place batting on top of the folded fabric. With batting side down, and leaving a 4″ opening for turning, use a ½″ seam to stitch all raw edges. Turn and slipstitch opening closed. Topstitch the belt ½″ from all edges. Measure in another ½″ and repeat, for 4 rows of topstitching. Center Velcro on each end of belt, where it will overlap to fit the waist, and hand-stitch Velcro to belt.

POINSETTIA CARD HOLDER

Materials:
    chart and color key on page 147
    stitch diagrams on page 147
    2 sheets #7 mesh plastic canvas
    #16 tapestry needle
    worsted-weight yarn: 2 yards gold, 3 yards dark green, 6 yards light green, 6 yards medium red, 14 yards dark red, 27 yards black, and 32 yards light red
    ¼ yard red felt (for lining)

From plastic canvas cut two 5¼″ x 7½″ pieces for front and back, two 3⅝″ x 5¼″ pieces for sides, and a 3½″ x 7½″ piece for the bottom. Using canvas pieces as patterns, cut out same pieces from red felt as above, except cut 2 bottom pieces.

Using a half-cross stitch, work charted design on front and back, filling in entire background area with black yarn (disregard slots for belt). Use 1 strand of black yarn for backstitching lines. Work sides in rows of slanted gobelin stitch with the light red yarn. Leave bottom piece unworked.

To finish, sew the canvas pieces together with black yarn and an overcast stitch. Cover top raw edge with overcast stitch, taking 2-3 stitches in the corners for best coverage.

Glue felt pieces inside box, covering all stitching but the top overcast stitching. Glue felt piece to bottom of box.

Food Jar Finery

Do you like to tickle the taste buds of kith and kin with gifts of home cooking? This year, bring a smile to faces even before that first delicious bite. Package your canned goods in jars that sport a cross-stitched chef's hat, and stuff sweets in containers protected by cinnamon bears that are all heart. Long after the jar contents have vanished, these fuzzy bears will radiate a savory scent.

CHEF'S HAT JAR TOPPER

Materials:
   chart on page 149
   graph paper
   white 14-count Aida trim, ⅞" wide, 1" longer than diameter of jar lid
   mason jar
   6-strand embroidery floss
   white thread
   9½" square piece of white broadcloth
   hot glue gun or fabric glue

Using the charted alphabet and graph paper, make a stitch diagram of the wording for jar topper. Leave 1 square between letters of a word and 3 squares between words. Fold graphed wording in half to find and mark midpoint.

Cut a strip of Aida trim to fit around lid of jar with a 1" overlap. (If desired, substitute a strip ⅞"-wide cut from Aida cloth and bound with satin stitches.) On the center of strip, stitch message, using 3 strands of embroidery floss in any color desired. There will be 2 rows of unworked fabric above and below the lettering.

When stitchery is complete, wrap strip around metal band of jar lid. Fold end under ¼", and then over other end. Adjust strip to fit snugly, allowing sufficient ease to slip the fabric off and on. Remove from band and whipstitch ends together.

Cut a circle 9½" in diameter from the white broadcloth. Stitch 2 rows of gathering stitches ⅛" from the outer edge, ⅛" apart. Gather to fit inside the cross-stitched band. Secure thread ends and even gathers. Glue hat crown inside band so that the band covers stitching. Allow to dry, and then slip finished hat over metal jar top ring. (Glue in place, if desired.) Screw cap on jar.

CINNAMON BEAR JARS

Materials:
   pattern on page 149
   glass containers
   silicone glue
   coarsely ground cinnamon
   craft heart appliqués, ⅜" and ⅞"
   ⅛"-wide blue satin ribbon
   blue-and-white check cotton fabric
   medium weight iron-on interfacing
   pinking shears
   ⅔ yard of cord style elastic
   matching thread
   glue

Transfer pattern to the jar. Trace one or several equally spaced bears onto jars, as

desired. Fill in traced area with silicone glue and cover completely with the cinnamon. Glue hearts on each side of bears as shown in photo. Cut 4" lengths of ribbon, tie into small bows, and glue to the necks of bears.

To top a 1-quart jar, cut a 9½"-diameter circle from the fabric and the interfacing. (Adjust size of topper to suit jar.) Iron to fuse the interfacing to the wrong side of the fabric. Trim edges with pinking shears. Encase elastic 1" from edge of circle, on interfacing side, with a zigzag stitch. Pull the ends of the elastic to fit jar, and tie ends securely. Even gathers and slip on jar. Make a bow with 8" of ribbon, and glue to the jar topper. Glue a large heart on the bow.

Warm the Hearts of Bread Lovers

A crisp white cloth, delicately cross-stitched with the bright red and green colors of the season, is sure to be one of those little touches that friends will remember.

The simplicity of the design is part of the charm. And when stitched on Salem cloth, which contains a bit of polyester, the bread cloth may also be machine washed.

Present it wrapped around a loaf of bread, a batch of cookies, or simply as a gift in itself covered with tissue paper and ribbon. Each time it is used, friends will remember your thoughtfulness.

Materials:
   chart and color key on page 149
   18″ square of 14-count Aida or Salem cloth
   embroidery floss (see color chart)

Ravel edges of the cloth to a ½″ margin on all sides. To prevent further raveling, machine-stitch along inner edge of fringe.

For word placement, begin the count from the corner of cloth. Using 2 strands of floss for all stitching, work design on cloth according to chart.

Celebrations from the Kitchen

Revel in the spirit of Christmas. The holidays are here and it's time to create new memories—to gather family and friends and to pamper them with delicious foods. Every meal doesn't have to be the fancy sit-down kind, but with the recipes we offer you here, each will be outstanding. Multiply the merrymaking (and divide the work) with a progressive dinner that travels to a different home with each course. Glorify holiday cakes and sauces with the zing of citrus. Wake the family with the irresistible aroma of coffee cakes and sweet breads. Titillate taste buds with scrumptious party fare and desserts. But most of all, make it festive and make it fun.

Christmas with Citrus Flavor

Long favored for rich color, piquant flavor, and abundant vitamins and minerals, citrus fruit holds a time-honored position in Christmas celebrations. Oranges, grapefruit, lemons, and limes come to full ripeness in the heart of winter, bringing sunny warmth to an often-cold and gray time of year. Reap a bounty of citrus goodness with concoctions that include Glazed Orange Ham, Broccoli with Lemon-Basil Sauce, Orange Layer Cake, and Cranberry-Orange Chutney.

LIME CREAM

2 envelopes unflavored gelatin
1 cup milk
8 egg yolks
1 cup sugar
1 quart half-and-half
2 to 3 teaspoons grated lime rind
½ cup lime juice
   Lime slices (optional)
   Lime rind (optional)

Soften gelatin in milk; let stand 5 minutes.
  Beat egg yolks and sugar at medium-high speed of an electric mixer until thick and lemon colored. Add half-and-half; mix well. Cook over low heat, stirring constantly, until mixture thickens and coats a spoon (about 10 minutes). Remove from heat; add gelatin mixture, stirring until gelatin dissolves. Gradually stir in lime rind and lime juice; cool. Pour into a lightly oiled 8-cup mold; chill 8 hours. Unmold on serving platter. Garnish with lime slices and rind, if desired. Yield: 10 servings.

Molded Lime Cream is a smooth finish for a rich holiday repast.

CREAMY ORANGE SALAD

1 (8½-ounce) can crushed pineapple, undrained
4 medium navel oranges, peeled and sectioned
1 (3-ounce) package orange-flavored gelatin
1 cup boiling water
1 (8-ounce) carton commercial sour cream
1 cup flaked coconut
1 cup chopped pecans
   Lettuce leaves

Drain pineapple, reserving liquid; set aside.
  Chop the orange sections; drain and then set aside.
  Dissolve gelatin in boiling water; cool. Add sour cream and pineapple juice, stirring well; chill until mixture is the consistency of unbeaten egg white. Stir in pineapple, oranges, coconut, and pecans; pour into a lightly oiled 4-cup mold or individual molds. Cover and chill until firm. Unmold salad on lettuce leaves. Yield: 8 servings.

CRANBERRY-ORANGE CHUTNEY

2 oranges, peeled and sectioned
1 (16-ounce) can whole-berry cranberry sauce
1 (16-ounce) can pear halves, drained and chopped
1 apple, unpeeled and chopped
1 cup sugar
½ cup raisins
¼ cup chopped pecans
1 tablespoon vinegar
½ teaspoon ground ginger
½ teaspoon ground cinnamon

Combine all ingredients in a saucepan; bring to a boil over medium heat. Reduce heat, and simmer 5 minutes. Let cool. Store in refrigerator. Yield: 5 cups.

ORANGE LAYER CAKE

½ cup butter or margarine, softened
1½ cups sugar
2 egg yolks
1 tablespoon grated orange rind
2¼ cups all-purpose flour
2 teaspoons baking powder
¼ teaspoon baking soda
½ teaspoon salt
¾ cup milk
¼ cup orange juice
4 egg whites
    Orange Filling
    Orange Buttercream Frosting

Cream butter; gradually add sugar, beating well at medium speed of an electric mixer. Add egg yolks, one at a time, beating after each addition. Stir in orange rind.

Combine flour, baking powder, soda, and salt. Combine milk and orange juice. Add the flour mixture to the creamed mixture alternately with liquid, beginning and ending with the flour mixture. Mix well after each addition.

Beat egg whites (at room temperature) until stiff peaks form; fold into batter. Pour batter into 2 greased and floured 8-inch round cakepans. Bake at 350° for 25 to 30 minutes or until a wooden pick inserted in center comes out clean. Cool in pans 10 minutes; remove layers from pans, and let cool completely on wire racks. Spread Orange Filling between layers. Spread Orange Buttercream Frosting on top and sides of cake. Yield: one 2-layer cake.

Orange Filling:

½ cup sugar
2 tablespoons cornstarch
¼ teaspoon salt
¾ cup orange juice
¼ cup water
2 egg yolks, slightly beaten
2 tablespoons butter or margarine
1½ teaspoons grated orange rind

Combine first 3 ingredients in a small saucepan; mix well. Gradually add orange juice, water, and egg yolks. Cook over medium heat, stirring constantly, until mixture comes to a boil. Cook 1 minute. Remove from heat; stir in butter and orange rind. Cool. Yield: 1¼ cups.

Orange Buttercream Frosting:

¼ cup plus 2 tablespoons butter, softened
1 (16 ounce) package powdered sugar, sifted
4 to 6 tablespoons orange juice
1 tablespoon grated orange rind

Cream butter; add powdered sugar alternately with orange juice. Add orange rind, beating until smooth. Yield: 2 cups.

ORANGE BALLS

9 medium oranges
2 cups sugar
¾ cup water
½ cup butter or margarine
1 (24-ounce) package chocolate almond bark, melted

Peel oranges, leaving membrane on fruit. Cut peel into strips. Reserve orange sections for other uses. Place peel in a medium saucepan; cover with water and cook 1 hour or until tender. Finely chop and measure enough orange peel to make 2 cups.

Combine 2 cups peel, sugar, ¾ cup water, and butter in a heavy saucepan. Cook over medium heat, stirring frequently, until mixture reaches 200° (mixture will be very thick). Remove orange mixture from heat and let cool. Shape into ¾-inch balls.

Place almond bark in top of a double boiler; bring water to a boil. Reduce heat to low; cook until melted. Dip orange balls in melted almond bark. Place on waxed paper to cool. Yield: about 7 dozen.

BROCCOLI WITH LEMON-BASIL SAUCE

  1 (1½-pound) bunch fresh broccoli
  1 egg, beaten
  ½ cup butter
  1 teaspoon grated lemon rind
  ¼ cup lemon juice
  ¼ teaspoon dried whole basil
    Lemon twists (optional)

Trim off broccoli leaves. Remove ends of stalks; wash broccoli thoroughly. Cook, covered, in a small amount of boiling water 8 to 10 minutes or until tender; drain, and arrange on serving platter. Keep warm.

Combine egg and butter in top of a double boiler; bring water to a boil. Cook until butter melts and mixture begins to thicken. Add lemon rind, lemon juice, and basil; cook, stirring constantly, an additional 2 minutes or until slightly thickened. Pour over broccoli. Garnish with lemon twists, if desired. Yield: 6 servings.

GLAZED ORANGE HAM

  1 (3-pound) fully cooked ham slice
    (about 2 inches thick)
  2 oranges, cut into ½-inch slices
  ¼ cup firmly packed brown sugar
  ½ teaspoon ground cinnamon
  ½ teaspoon ground cloves
  ½ teaspoon ground allspice
  ¼ teaspoon pepper
  ½ cup orange juice
    Maraschino cherries, halved
    (optional)

Place ham in a lightly greased 12- x 8- x 2-inch baking dish; top with orange slices. Combine brown sugar and seasonings; sprinkle mixture over oranges. Pour orange juice over ham. Cover, and bake at 350° for 1 hour. Uncover, and bake an additional 15 minutes or until thermometer registers 140°, basting frequently. Garnish with maraschino cherries, if desired. Yield: 8 servings.

This family has the advantage of being able to select fresh citrus fruit in December at one of the sources, Blood's Hammock Groves in Delray Beach, Florida. When choosing any citrus, look for firm, unblemished fruit that is heavy for its size. Don't be put off by green color that may appear on oranges—citrus fruit is only picked when ripe. Weather can change skin color, but that doesn't affect the ripeness of the fruit itself. Once purchased, citrus fruit will remain fresh in your refrigerator for as long as two months.

A Dinner Party on the Move

Transform a holiday gathering into a roving, rollicking good time. This year try spreading out both the cheer and the work with a progressive dinner. Moving from place to place provides a sense of adventure; dishes like Royal Seafood Tarts, Green Pepper Soup, and Gingered Peach Salad create a gustatory sensation. The recipes that follow are ready to be divided among your fellow diners.

Herb Cheese Balls
Royal Seafood Tarts
White Wine

Green Pepper Soup
Soft Rye Breadsticks

Champagne Ice
Holiday Entrée
Spinach Pom-Poms
Gingered Peach Salad
Sour Cream Dinner Rolls
White Wine

White Chocolate Dessert
Coffee
(Menu serves 12.)

Above right: A progressive dinner keeps holiday entertaining from being a burden for any one cook. It also lets friends enjoy each other's decorations between courses.

Right: Green Pepper Soup in a mug and Soft Rye Breadsticks are wonderfully portable, making it easy to move about and talk.

Opposite: When it's time to draw up a chair, the selection includes Holiday Entrée (made with chicken, ham, and spices), Spinach Pom-Poms, and Sour Cream Dinner Rolls.

HERB CHEESE BALLS

2 (8-ounce) packages cream cheese, softened
1 (8-ounce) container whipped butter, softened
2 cloves garlic, minced
½ teaspoon dried whole oregano
¼ teaspoon dried whole basil
¼ teaspoon dill weed
¼ teaspoon dried whole marjoram
¼ teaspoon pepper
¼ teaspoon dried whole thyme
  Coarsely ground black pepper or lemon-pepper seasoning

Combine all ingredients, except coarsely ground black pepper, in a large mixing bowl; beat at medium speed of an electric mixer until smooth. Chill 12 hours.

Shape mixture into 2 (3-inch) balls, coating with coarsely ground black pepper; serve with crackers. Yield: about 3½ cups.

Note: Mixture can be spooned into a decorating bag fitted with a tip, piped onto crackers, and sprinkled with coarsely ground black pepper.

ROYAL SEAFOOD TARTS

1 (8-ounce) package frozen cooked shrimp, thawed and drained
¼ cup chopped mushrooms
1 tablespoon butter or margarine, melted
½ cup commercial sour cream
½ cup (2 ounces) shredded Swiss cheese
1 tablespoon tomato paste
1 tablespoon lemon juice
1 teaspoon Worcestershire sauce
½ teaspoon prepared horseradish
⅛ teaspoon pepper
  Tart shells (recipe follows)

Set aside 24 whole shrimp; chop remaining shrimp. Sauté mushrooms in butter in a large skillet until tender; drain.

Stir in chopped shrimp and the next 7 ingredients; then cook over low heat until the mixture is thoroughly heated. Spoon the mixture into baked tart shells. Bake the tarts at 400° for 5 to 10 minutes.

Top each tart with a reserved whole shrimp, and bake the tarts an additional 5 minutes. Yield: 2 dozen.

Tart Shells:

1½ cups all-purpose flour
½ teaspoon salt
½ cup shortening
3 to 4 tablespoons cold water

Combine flour and salt; cut in shortening with a pastry blender until mixture resembles coarse meal.

Sprinkle water, 1 tablespoon at a time, evenly over surface, and stir with a fork until all of the ingredients are moistened. Chill. Divide dough into 24 (1-inch) balls. Place the balls in individual wells of ungreased 1¾-inch muffin pans, pressing dough onto the bottom and sides to form shells. Bake the shells at 425° for 10 minutes or until lightly browned. Yield: 2 dozen.

GREEN PEPPER SOUP

2 large green peppers, chopped
2 large onions, chopped
¼ cup butter or margarine, melted
4 (10½-ounce) cans chicken broth, undiluted and divided
¼ cup butter or margarine
¼ cup all-purpose flour
4 cups milk
½ to 1 teaspoon dried whole oregano
½ teaspoon white pepper

Sauté green pepper and onion in ¼ cup butter until tender. Combine half of vegetable mixture and half of broth in container of an electric blender; process until smooth. Repeat procedure with remaining vegetable mixture and broth. Set aside.

Melt ¼ cup butter in a large Dutch oven over low heat; add flour, stirring until smooth. Cook 1 minute, stirring constantly. Gradually add milk; cook over medium heat, stirring constantly, until mixture is thickened and bubbly. Stir in oregano, pepper, and vegetable mixture. Cook over medium heat until soup begins to boil, stirring frequently. Chill. (Soup may be served hot, if desired.) Yield: 10 cups.

SOFT RYE BREADSTICKS

    1 package dry yeast
    ¼ cup warm water (105° to 115°)
    3 tablespoons molasses
    1 teaspoon salt
    2 teaspoons caraway seeds
    3 tablespoons butter or margarine,
         melted
    1 cup lukewarm water
 1¾ cups rye flour
 1½ to 2½ cups all-purpose flour
    1 egg yolk, beaten
         Caraway seeds

Dissolve yeast in ¼ cup warm water in a large mixing bowl; let stand 5 minutes. Add molasses and next 5 ingredients; beat at medium speed of an electric mixer 2 minutes. Gradually stir in enough all-purpose flour to form a stiff dough.

Turn dough out onto a lightly floured surface, and knead until smooth and elastic (about 5 to 10 minutes). Place in a greased bowl, turning to grease top. Cover and let rise in a warm place (85°), free from drafts, 1 hour or until doubled in bulk.

Punch dough down, and divide in half. Divide each half into 24 equal pieces. Roll each piece of dough into a 6-inch long rope. Place on lightly greased baking sheets. Cover and let rise in a warm place (85°), free from drafts, 30 minutes.

Brush the dough with egg yolk, and sprinkle it with caraway seeds. Bake at 400° for 10 to 15 minutes. Remove breadsticks from baking sheets, and cool them on wire racks. Yield: 4 dozen.

CHAMPAGNE ICE

 1½ cups sugar
    3 cups water
         Grated rind of 3 lemons
         Juice of 3 lemons
    6 cups champagne

Combine sugar and water in a small saucepan; bring to a boil, stirring constantly. Cover, reduce heat, and simmer 5 minutes. Let cool.

Combine sugar mixture, lemon rind, lemon juice, and champagne. Then pour mixture into a 13- x 9- x 2-inch pan. Freeze it until almost firm. Spoon mixture into a bowl, and beat at medium speed of an electric mixer until slushy. Return to pan. Freeze mixture for 8 hours. Spoon mixture into sherbet glasses and serve immediately. Yield: 10 cups.

Tip: When you use fresh lemons for cooking, remember that one medium lemon will yield 2 to 4 tablespoons juice and 1 tablespoon grated rind. Before cutting, roll lemons, oranges, and grapefruit on a counter to soften; you will get more juice. When squeezing fresh lemons or oranges for juice, first grate the rind by rubbing the washed fruit against surface of grater, taking care to remove only the outer colored portion of the rind. Wrap in plastic in teaspoon portions and freeze for future use.

HOLIDAY ENTRÉE

12 chicken breast halves, skinned
   and boned
¾ cup all-purpose flour
½ cup butter or margarine, melted
3 (¼-inch thick) center-cut ham
   slices (about 3 pounds)
½ cup vegetable oil
¼ cup plus 2 tablespoons vinegar
¼ cup dry white wine
2½ tablespoons sugar
1½ tablespoons paprika
2 teaspoons salt
½ teaspoon red pepper
3 small cloves garlic, crushed
12 small-to-medium size new
   potatoes

Place each chicken breast half between 2
sheets of waxed paper; flatten to ½-inch
thickness, using a meat mallet or rolling pin.
Dredge chicken with flour; brown in butter
in a heavy skillet. Set aside.

Cut each ham slice into 4 serving-size
pieces; place ham pieces in two lightly
greased 12- x 8- x 2-inch baking dishes. Top
each ham slice with a chicken breast.

Combine vegetable oil and next 7 ingredients, mixing well; pour mixture over
chicken. Cover and chill 8 hours.

Wash potatoes, and pat dry. Cut each
potato into ¼-inch slices, cutting crosswise
and to, but not through, bottom of potato.
(Cut potato should resemble a fan.) Allow
potatoes to stand in ice water 5 minutes to
open slices. Drain well, and place 6 potatoes
in each baking dish.

Cover and bake at 350° for 1 hour, basting
frequently with marinade. Yield: 12 servings.

SPINACH POM-POMS

2 (10-ounce) packages frozen
   chopped spinach, thawed and
   drained
2 cups herb-seasoned stuffing mix,
   crushed
1 cup grated Parmesan cheese
6 eggs, beaten
½ cup butter or margarine, softened
   Dash of ground nutmeg
   Sweet red pepper rings (optional)
   Spicy Mustard Sauce

Place spinach on paper towels, and squeeze
until barely moist. Combine spinach and
next 5 ingredients in a bowl; mix well. Shape
into 2½-inch balls with an ice cream scoop;
place on a waxed paper-lined baking sheet.
Cover and refrigerate 8 hours.

To bake, place spinach balls on a lightly
greased baking sheet, and bake at 350° for 15
minutes or until hot. Drain on paper towels.
Place on red pepper rings, if desired. Serve
with Spicy Mustard Sauce. Yield: 15 servings.

Spicy Mustard Sauce:

⅓ to ½ cup dry mustard
½ cup white vinegar
½ cup sugar
1 egg yolk

Combine mustard and vinegar in a small
bowl; blend well. Cover and let stand at
room temperature 8 hours.

Combine mustard mixture, sugar, and egg
yolk in a small saucepan. Cook over low heat
until slightly thickened, stirring occasionally. Cover and store in refrigerator. Serve at
room temperature. Yield: ¾ cup.

*Tip: Unused or extra egg whites freeze well
and may be used as needed. Make meringues
or angel pies with whites that are leftover.*

GINGERED PEACH SALAD

1 (3-ounce) package orange-flavored gelatin
1 (3-ounce) package lemon-flavored gelatin
1 cup boiling water
1 (29-ounce) jar spiced peaches, undrained
1 (8-ounce) can crushed pineapple, undrained
1 tablespoon lemon juice
1 tablespoon orange juice
1 teaspoon ground ginger
½ teaspoon salt
½ cup chopped celery
½ cup chopped pecans
Lettuce leaves
½ cup commercial sour cream
¼ teaspoon ground ginger
Celery leaves

Dissolve gelatin in boiling water. Drain peaches and pineapple, reserving 1¾ cups juice; set aside. Chop peaches; set aside. Combine gelatin, reserved juice, and next 4 ingredients; stir until well blended. Add celery, pecans, peaches, and pineapple, mixing well. Pour into a lightly oiled 9-inch square dish. Cover and chill until firm. Serve on lettuce leaves. Combine sour cream and ginger; spoon 1 teaspoon on each serving. Top with celery leaves. Yield: 12 servings.

SOUR CREAM DINNER ROLLS

2 packages dry yeast
½ cup warm water (105° to 115°)
1 cup milk
½ cup commercial sour cream
½ cup butter or margarine
½ cup sugar
2 eggs, beaten
2 teaspoons salt
5½ to 6 cups all-purpose flour, divided
½ cup butter or margarine, softened and divided

Dissolve yeast in warm water in a large mixing bowl; let stand 5 minutes. Heat milk and next 3 ingredients. Cool to 105° to 115°. Add milk mixture, eggs, salt, and 2 cups flour to yeast; beat at medium speed of an electric mixer 2 minutes. Stir in enough flour to make a medium-stiff dough. In a well-greased bowl, turn to grease top, cover, and refrigerate overnight.

Turn dough out onto a floured surface, and knead 1 minute or until smooth and elastic. Divide dough into 4 portions. Roll one portion of dough into a 12-inch circle on a lightly floured surface. Spread 2 tablespoons butter over dough. Cut into 12 wedges; roll each wedge tightly, beginning at wide end. Seal points, and place about 2 inches apart on a greased baking sheet, curving into crescent shapes. Cover and let rise in a warm place (85°), free from drafts, 45 minutes or until doubled in bulk. Continue process with remaining dough and butter. Bake at 375° for 15 to 20 minutes or until golden brown. Yield: 4 dozen.

WHITE CHOCOLATE DESSERT

3 egg whites
½ cup sugar
23 round buttery crackers, crumbled
2 cups whipping cream
¼ cup sifted powdered sugar
¾ teaspoon vanilla extract
½ teaspoon almond extract
½ pound white chocolate, grated

Beat egg whites (at room temperature) until foamy. Gradually add sugar, 1 tablespoon at a time, beating until stiff peaks form. Fold in cracker crumbs. Pour mixture into a lightly greased 13- x 9- x 2-inch baking dish. Bake at 325° for 25 minutes. Cool 2 hours.

Beat whipping cream until foamy; gradually add powdered sugar, beating until soft peaks form. Stir in flavorings. Spread mixture over crust. Sprinkle with chocolate. Chill. Yield: 12 to 15 servings.

Invite Friends to a Holiday Luncheon

In the throes of the holiday season, even the most active woman can find preparing lunch for guests taxing, to say the least. Whether you plan to entertain a social or professional group or you just want to have some friends over while the kids are still in school, the key to success is to make dishes ahead of time and then quickly pull them together before your company arrives.

Shrimp Mousse
Crackers
Beef Tenderloin
Angel Biscuits
Creamy Horseradish Mustard
Marinated Asparagus with Pecans
Christmas Salad
Amaretto Crème Brûlée
(Menu serves 10-12.)

Above: Baskets, filled with food that can wait, decorate the buffet while guests gather, then make serving easy and stylish.

SHRIMP MOUSSE

    2 envelopes unflavored gelatin
    ¼ cup cold water
    1 (8-ounce) package cream cheese, softened
    ¾ cup commercial sour cream
    ¼ cup mayonnaise
    ¼ cup chili sauce
    2 tablespoons lemon juice
    ½ teaspoon salt
    ½ teaspoon Worcestershire sauce
    ¼ teaspoon hot sauce
    2 (8-ounce) packages frozen cooked shrimp, thawed and diced
    ¼ cup diced green pepper
    ¼ cup diced celery
    2 tablespoons diced pimiento
      Leaf lettuce

Sprinkle gelatin over water in a small saucepan; place over low heat, stirring until gelatin dissolves. Set aside.

Combine gelatin mixture, cream cheese, and next 7 ingredients in a mixing bowl; beat at medium speed of an electric mixer until smooth. Stir in shrimp, green pepper, celery, and pimiento.

Pour into a lightly oiled 6-cup mold; chill until firm. Unmold on a lettuce-lined serving plate. Serve mousse with assorted crackers. Yield: 4⅔ cups.

Treat guests to slices of Beef Tenderloin in Angel Biscuits, Christmas Salad, and Marinated Asparagus with Pecans—all served in baskets lined with pretty linens.

BEEF TENDERLOIN

  1 (4½-pound) beef tenderloin,
      trimmed
 ¼ cup plus 2 tablespoons olive oil
  3 tablespoons soy sauce
  2 teaspoons seasoned salt
 ¼ teaspoon pepper
 ⅛ teaspoon garlic powder
 ⅛ teaspoon dried whole thyme

Trim excess fat from tenderloin. Place tenderloin in a large shallow dish.

Combine olive oil and next 5 ingredients, mixing well. Pour marinade over tenderloin; cover with foil and refrigerate 8 hours, turning occasionally.

Remove tenderloin from marinade. Place tenderloin on a rack in a baking pan; insert meat thermometer. Bake at 425° for 30 to 45 minutes or until thermometer registers 140° (rare). Bake until thermometer registers 150° for medium-rare or 160° for medium. Cool and slice.

Spread Angel Biscuits with Creamy Horseradish Mustard and fill with sliced tenderloin. Yield: enough to fill 3½ dozen biscuits.

ANGEL BISCUITS

  2 packages dry yeast
  2 tablespoons sugar
 ¼ cup lukewarm water (105° to 115°)
  5 cups self-rising flour
  1 teaspoon salt
  1 teaspoon baking soda
 ¾ cup shortening
  2 cups buttermilk

Dissolve yeast and sugar in warm water; let stand 5 minutes.

Combine flour, salt, and soda; mix well. Cut in shortening with a pastry blender until mixture resembles coarse meal. Add yeast mixture and buttermilk, stirring until dry ingredients are moistened.

Turn dough out onto a floured surface, and knead until smooth and elastic (about 8 to 10 minutes). Roll dough to ¼-inch thickness. Cut with a 2½-inch biscuit cutter, and place ½ inch apart on lightly greased baking sheets. Bake at 450° for 10 to 12 minutes. Yield: 3½ dozen.

Note: Dough may be stored in refrigerator up to 1 week.

CREAMY HORSERADISH MUSTARD

 ¾ cup half-and-half, divided
  1 egg yolk, beaten
 ⅓ cup sugar
  2 tablespoons all-purpose flour
 ¼ teaspoon salt
  3 tablespoons creole mustard
 ¼ cup white wine vinegar
  1 tablespoon prepared horseradish

Scald ¼ cup half-and-half in a small saucepan. Set aside.

Combine egg yolk, ½ cup half-and-half, sugar, flour, salt, and mustard. Gradually add to scalded half-and-half; cook over low heat, stirring constantly, 10 minutes or until thickened. Stir in vinegar and horseradish. Store in refrigerator. Yield: 1⅓ cups.

MARINATED ASPARAGUS WITH PECANS

   3 pounds fresh asparagus
 ½ cup cider vinegar
 ¼ cup soy sauce
 ¼ cup vegetable oil
 ¼ cup sugar
 ⅛ teaspoon pepper
1¼ cups chopped pecans
   2 tablespoons butter or margarine,
       melted

Remove tough ends of asparagus. Remove scales from stalks with a knife or vegetable peeler, and cut into 2-inch pieces. Cook, covered, in boiling water 6 to 8 minutes or until crisp-tender; drain.

Combine vinegar, soy sauce, vegetable oil, sugar, and pepper in a jar; cover tightly, and shake vigorously. Place asparagus in a shallow container; pour marinade over asparagus. Cover and chill 8 hours. Drain. Spoon into individual dishes.

Sauté pecans in butter until brown. Sprinkle over asparagus. Yield: 10 to 12 servings.

CHRISTMAS SALAD

   2 eggs
 ¼ cup plus 2 tablespoons sugar
   3 tablespoons white wine vinegar
   2 tablespoons butter or margarine,
       melted
   1 cup whipping cream, whipped
   1 (20-ounce) can pineapple chunks
       drained
   1 (16½-ounce) can pitted Royal Anne
       cherries, drained
   2 cups seedless red grapes, halved
1½ cups miniature marshmallows

Combine eggs and sugar in a small saucepan; beat well with wire whisk. Add vinegar and butter; cook over low heat, stirring constantly, until smooth and thickened. Cool. Fold in whipped cream.

Combine fruits and marshmallows; fold in dressing. Chill at least 3 hours. Spoon into individual dishes. Yield: 12 servings.

AMARETTO CRÈME BRÛLÉE

 ¼ cup firmly packed brown sugar,
       divided
   1 (14-ounce) can sweetened
       condensed milk
   4 cups hot water
   6 eggs
   2 tablespoons amaretto
       Whipped cream (optional)
       Sliced almonds, toasted (optional)
       Amaretto (optional)

Place 1 teaspoon brown sugar in each of 12 (6-ounce) custard cups; set aside.

Combine condensed milk and water, stirring well; set aside.

Beat eggs in a large mixing bowl until frothy; gradually add milk mixture, mixing well. Stir in 2 tablespoons amaretto.

Pour mixture into custard cups. Place cups in two 13- x 9- x 2-inch baking pans. Pour hot water into pans to a depth of 1 inch. Bake at 325° for 50 minutes or until a knife inserted in the center comes out clean. Remove cups from water, and cool. Chill.

To serve, loosen edges of custard with a spatula; quickly invert onto dessert plates. Garnish with whipped cream and almonds, and drizzle with amaretto, if desired. Yield: 12 servings.

Tip: When cooking for a crowd, plan your menu so that you can use several cooking appliances in addition to your oven. Don't forget to use the stove top, microwave, electric skillet, and toaster oven.

Breads

MAPLE BUTTER COFFEE CAKE

¾ cup milk
¼ cup butter or margarine
3½ to 3¾ cups all-purpose flour, divided
3 tablespoons sugar
1 package dry yeast
½ teaspoon salt
2 eggs, beaten
½ cup firmly packed brown sugar
2 tablespoons all-purpose flour
½ teaspoon ground cinnamon
¼ cup butter or margarine, softened
¼ cup maple syrup
½ cup chopped pecans
1½ cups sifted powdered sugar
2 tablespoons butter or margarine, softened
3 tablespoons milk
½ teaspoon vanilla extract
Candied green and red cherries

Combine ¾ cup milk and ¼ cup butter in a small saucepan; heat until very warm (120° to 130°). Set aside.

Combine 1½ cups flour, sugar, yeast, and salt in a large bowl; stir well. Gradually add milk mixture to flour mixture, stirring well; add eggs. Beat at medium speed of an electric mixer until smooth. Gradually stir in enough of remaining 2 to 2¼ cups flour to make a stiff dough. Cover and let rise in a warm place (85°), free from drafts, for 1½ hours.

Punch dough down, and divide in half. Roll half of dough into an 18- x 8-inch rectangle on a lightly floured surface. Combine brown sugar, 2 tablespoons flour, cinnamon, ¼ cup butter, maple syrup, and pecans, mixing well; spread half of mixture over rectangle. Beginning at long side, roll up jellyroll fashion; press edges and ends together securely. Place roll in a lightly greased 9-inch round cakepan; shape into a circle, pinching ends together. Gently flatten

Freshly baked breads will lure your family out of bed on even the coldest December morning. This spread includes (clockwise from bottom) Currant Scones, Cranberry-Walnut Streusel Muffins, and Maple Butter Coffee Cake.

with fingertips. Repeat procedure with remaining dough and filling mixture.

Cover and let rise in a warm place (85°), free from drafts, about 1 hour or until doubled in bulk. Bake at 350° for 25 to 30 minutes or until golden brown.

Combine powdered sugar, 2 tablespoons butter, 3 tablespoons milk, and vanilla. Beat at medium speed of an electric mixer until smooth. Drizzle over warm coffee cakes. Garnish with candied cherries. Yield: 2 coffee cakes.

Summon the richness of the Old World with cheese and whole wheat-rye breads twisted together and sprinkled with caraway and sesame seeds.

CHEESE-RYE TWISTS

1 package dry yeast
½ cup warm water (105° to 115°)
½ cup milk, scalded
3 tablespoons sugar
1½ teaspoons salt
1 tablespoon shortening
1 egg, slightly beaten
3 to 3½ cups all-purpose flour,
    divided
1 cup (4 ounces) shredded sharp
    Cheddar cheese
    Whole Wheat-Rye Bread
1 egg white, slightly beaten
    Sesame seeds
    Caraway seeds

Dissolve yeast in warm water in a large mixing bowl; let stand 5 minutes.

Combine milk, sugar, salt, and shortening, mixing well; cool to 105° to 115°. Add milk mixture, egg, and 1 cup flour to yeast mixture; beat at medium speed of an electric mixer. Stir in cheese; stir in enough remaining flour to make a soft dough.

Turn dough out onto a floured surface; cover and let rest 10 to 15 minutes. Knead dough until smooth and elastic (about 8 to 10 minutes). Place dough in a well-greased bowl, turning to grease top. Cover and let rise in a warm place (85°), free from drafts, 1 hour or until doubled in bulk.

Prepare Whole Wheat-Rye Bread. Divide each dough into 4 parts. Roll each part into a 17-inch rope. Place a cheese rope and a whole wheat-rye rope side by side on a lightly floured surface. Twist the two ropes together. Tuck ends under to seal. Place on a greased baking sheet. Repeat procedure with remaining dough.

Brush each twist with egg white. Sprinkle sesame seeds on cheese dough and caraway seeds on whole wheat-rye dough. Cover and let rise in a warm place (85°), free from drafts, for 1 hour or until doubled in bulk. Bake at 375° for 15 minutes. Remove to wire racks to cool. Yield: 4 loaves.

Whole Wheat-Rye Bread:

1 package dry yeast
¼ cup warm water (105° to 115°)
2½ tablespoons molasses
1½ teaspoons salt
1½ teaspoons caraway seeds
2 tablespoons shortening
¾ cup plus 2 tablespoons lukewarm
    water
¾ cup rye flour
¾ cup whole wheat flour
1½ to 2 cups all-purpose flour

Dissolve yeast in ¼ cup warm water in a large mixing bowl; let stand 5 minutes. Stir in next 7 ingredients; beat at medium speed of an electric mixer until smooth. Gradually stir in enough all-purpose flour to make a soft dough.

Turn dough out onto a floured surface, and knead until smooth and elastic (about 8 to 10 minutes). Place in a well-greased bowl, turning to grease top. Cover and let rise in a warm place (85°), free from drafts, 1 hour or until doubled in bulk.

SURPRISE BISCUITS

2 cups self-rising flour
1 teaspoon sugar
1 cup whipping cream
2 tablespoons raspberry, strawberry,
    or apricot preserves

Combine first 3 ingredients; mix well. (Dough will be stiff.) Turn out onto a floured surface, and knead 10 to 12 times.

Roll dough to ½-inch thickness; cut with a 2½-inch biscuit cutter. Make 6 slits through dough around edge of each biscuit to within ¼ inch of center. Place on lightly greased baking sheets. Press down center of each biscuit, making a dent with thumb. Spoon ½ teaspoon preserves into each center.

Bake at 450° for 10 minutes or until lightly browned. Yield: about 1 dozen.

CRANBERRY-WALNUT STREUSEL MUFFINS

```
2   cups all-purpose flour, divided
1   cup firmly packed brown sugar
½   cup butter or margarine
⅔   cup chopped walnuts, divided
2   teaspoons baking powder
½   teaspoon baking soda
½   teaspoon salt
1   teaspoon ground nutmeg
½   teaspoon grated orange rind
2   eggs, beaten
⅔   cup buttermilk
1   cup fresh cranberries
```

Combine 1 cup flour and sugar; cut in butter with a pastry blender until mixture resembles coarse meal. Reserve ½ cup flour mixture, and stir in 3 tablespoons walnuts; set aside for topping.

Combine the remaining flour mixture, the remaining 1 cup flour, the baking powder, soda, salt, nutmeg, and orange rind in a large bowl.

Combine the eggs and buttermilk, mixing well. Make a well in the center of the flour mixture; add the egg mixture, stirring just until moistened. Stir in the cranberries and remaining walnuts.

Spoon batter into greased muffin pans, filling half full. Sprinkle with reserved flour-walnut mixture. Bake at 350° for 20 to 25 minutes. Yield: 1½ dozen.

SOUR CREAM TWISTS

```
3½  cups all-purpose flour
1   teaspoon salt
1   cup butter-flavored shortening
1   package dry yeast
¼   cup warm water (105° to 115°)
¾   cup commercial sour cream
1   egg, beaten
2   egg yolks, beaten
1   teaspoon vanilla extract
¾   cup sugar
```

Combine the flour and salt in a large mixing bowl; cut in the butter-flavored shortening with a pastry blender until the mixture resembles coarse meal.

Dissolve yeast in warm water. Add yeast mixture, sour cream, egg, egg yolks, and vanilla to flour mixture; mix well. Chill 2 hours. (Dough does not rise.)

Roll half of dough into a 16- x 8-inch rectangle on a sugared surface. Fold long sides to center, overlapping ends. Sprinkle with sugar, and repeat procedure. Roll dough to ¼-inch thickness; cut into 4- x 1-inch strips. Twist ends of strips in opposite directions, stretching dough slightly. Place on ungreased baking sheets. Bake at 375° for 15 minutes or until lightly browned. Remove from baking sheets, and cool completely on a wire rack. Yield: 7 dozen.

JUMBO CINNAMON ROLLS

```
2     packages dry yeast
¾     cup warm water (105° to 115°)
1⅔    cups milk, scalded
¼     cup shortening
¼     cup sugar
2     teaspoons salt
6½ to 7 cups all-purpose flour, divided
¼     cup butter or margarine, softened
¾     cup firmly packed brown sugar
1½    teaspoons ground cinnamon
¾     cup chopped pecans or walnuts
      Glaze (recipe follows)
```

Dissolve yeast in warm water in a large mixing bowl; let stand 5 minutes.

Combine milk, shortening, sugar, and salt, mixing well; cool to 105° to 115°. Add milk mixture and 3 cups flour to yeast mixture, beating at medium speed of an electric mixer until smooth. Stir in enough remaining flour to form a soft dough.

Turn dough out onto a lightly floured surface, and knead until smooth and elastic (about 5 minutes). Place dough in a greased bowl, turning to grease top. Cover and let rise in a warm place (85°), free from drafts, about 1 hour or until doubled in bulk.

Punch dough down; roll into an 18- x 12-inch rectangle on a lightly floured surface. Spread with butter, and sprinkle with brown sugar, cinnamon, and pecans. Starting at long end, roll up jellyroll fashion. Cut roll into 18 (1-inch) slices; place on lightly greased baking sheets or in 2 lightly greased 9-inch square pans. Cover rolls and let rise in a warm place (85°), free from drafts, for 40 minutes.

Bake at 350° for 20 to 25 minutes or until golden brown. Drizzle with glaze while warm. Yield: 1½ dozen.

Glaze:

  2 **cups sifted powdered sugar**
  ¼ **cup butter or margarine, softened**
  ¼ **cup orange juice**
  ½ **teaspoon vanilla extract**
  ½ **teaspoon almond extract**

Combine all ingredients; beat at medium speed of an electric mixer until smooth. Yield: about ¾ cup.

CURRANT SCONES

  ½ **cup currants**
  3 **tablespoons brandy**
  2¼ **cups all-purpose flour**
  1 **teaspoon baking powder**
  ¼ **teaspoon baking soda**
  ½ **cup butter**
  1 **cup plus 1 tablespoon whipping cream, divided**
     Sugar

Combine currants and brandy in a small bowl; set aside.

Combine flour, baking powder, and soda, mixing well. Cut in butter with a pastry blender until mixture resembles coarse meal. Add 1 cup whipping cream, stirring just until dry ingredients are moistened. Stir in currants. Chill.

Turn dough out onto a lightly floured surface, and knead lightly 4 or 5 times. Roll dough to ½-inch thickness; cut with a 1-inch round cutter. Place scones on a lightly greased baking sheet. Brush tops with 1 tablespoon cream and sprinkle with sugar. Bake at 375° for 15 to 18 minutes or until lightly browned. Yield: about 6½ dozen.

CHERRY SWEET BREAD

  2½ **cups all-purpose flour**
  2 **teaspoons baking powder**
  ½ **teaspoon baking soda**
  1 **cup candied red cherries, chopped**
  1 **cup walnuts or pecans, chopped**
  ¾ **cup butter or margarine, softened**
  1 **cup sugar**
  2 **eggs**
  1 **cup orange juice**
     Sifted powdered sugar (optional)

Combine flour, baking powder, and soda; set aside 1 cup of mixture for dredging fruit.

Combine cherries and walnuts in a large bowl; mix well. Dredge mixture in 1 cup reserved flour mixture.

Cream butter; gradually add sugar, beating until light and fluffy. Add eggs, one at a time, beating at medium speed of an electric mixer after each addition. Add dry ingredients alternately with orange juice, beginning and ending with flour mixture. Fold in fruit mixture. Pour batter into a greased and floured 10-inch Bundt pan. Bake at 350° for 1 hour or until a wooden pick inserted in center comes out clean. Cool bread in pan 10 minutes; remove from pan, and cool completely on a wire rack. Sprinkle bread with powdered sugar, if desired. Yield: one 10-inch bread ring.

Beverages

WHITE WINE COOLER

- 2 quarts boiling water
- 3 quart-size tea bags
- 1 cup sugar
- 1 (6-ounce) can frozen orange juice concentrate, thawed and undiluted
- 1 (6-ounce) can frozen lemonade concentrate, thawed and undiluted
- 1 gallon dry white wine
- 3¼ cups Cognac
- ¼ cup grenadine syrup
- 4 (33.8-ounce) bottles club soda, chilled

Pour 2 quarts boiling water over tea bags; cover. Let stand 10 minutes. Discard bags. Stir in sugar, orange juice concentrate, and lemonade concentrate, mixing well. Add wine, Cognac, and grenadine syrup; chill. To serve, add club soda, stirring well. Yield: about 3 gallons.

WASSAIL

- Whole cloves
- 6 oranges
- 1 gallon apple cider
- ⅓ cup sugar
- 1 cup lemon juice
- 10 (2-inch) sticks cinnamon
- 2 cups vodka
- ¼ cup brandy

Insert cloves in oranges about ½ inch apart. Place oranges in a 15- x 10- x 1-inch jellyroll pan; bake at 350° for 30 minutes. Combine apple cider and sugar in a large Dutch oven; cook over medium heat until mixture simmers. Add lemon juice, cinnamon sticks, and oranges; cover and cook over low heat 30 minutes. Add vodka and brandy; stir well. Serve warm. Yield: 4½ quarts.

AMARETTO EGGNOG

- 1 dozen eggs, separated
- 1 cup sugar
- 2 cups amaretto
- 1 quart plus 2 cups milk
- 1 teaspoon ground nutmeg
- 1 cup whipping cream
- Ground nutmeg

Beat egg yolks in a large mixing bowl at medium speed of an electric mixer until foamy; gradually add sugar, beating until thick and lemon colored. Add amaretto, 1 tablespoon at a time, beating until blended. Chill 2 hours.

Add milk and 1 teaspoon nutmeg to yolk mixture, mixing until well blended. Set aside.

Beat egg whites (at room temperature) at high speed of an electric mixer until soft peaks form. Set aside.

Beat whipping cream until soft peaks form. Fold egg whites and whipped cream into yolk mixture. Sprinkle with additional nutmeg, if desired. Yield: 4½ quarts.

KAHLÚA-AMARETTO FREEZE

- 1 quart chocolate ice cream
- 2 cups half-and-half
- ¾ cup Kahlúa
- ¼ cup amaretto

Combine half of all ingredients in container of an electric blender; process until smooth. Pour mixture into a pitcher. Repeat procedure with remaining half of ingredients; add to pitcher. Pour into stemmed glasses and serve immediately. Yield: about 7 cups.

Toast the season with creamy eggnog flavored with amaretto.

MOCK CHAMPAGNE PUNCH

1 **cup sugar**
3 **cups water**
1 **(12-ounce) can frozen lemonade concentrate, thawed and undiluted**
2 **cups sparkling Catawba, chilled**
2 **(33.8-ounce) bottles ginger ale, chilled**

Combine sugar and water in a saucepan; bring to a boil. Remove from heat, and cool. Stir in lemonade concentrate.

To serve, add Catawba and ginger ale, mixing well. Yield: about 4 quarts.

PERKY PUNCH

3 **cups pineapple juice**
3 **cups cranberry juice**
1½ **cups water**
½ **to ¾ cup firmly packed brown sugar**
1½ **teaspoons whole cloves**
1 **(3-inch) stick cinnamon**

Pour juices and water into an electric percolator; add brown sugar. Place cloves and cinnamon in the percolator basket. Perk through complete cycle; serve hot. Yield: about 2 quarts.

SPICED APPLE CIDER

2 **quarts apple cider**
3 **cups unsweetened pineapple juice**
¾ **cup orange juice**
2 **tablespoons lemon juice**
1 **teaspoon whole cloves**
½ **teaspoon whole allspice**
Rind of 1 orange, cut into strips

Combine first 4 ingredients in a Dutch oven. Tie cloves, allspice, and orange rind in a cheesecloth bag; add to cider mixture. Cook over medium heat until thoroughly heated. Remove spice bag. Serve hot or cold. Yield: about 3 quarts.

SPICED COFFEE

6 **cups cold water**
4 **(3-inch) sticks cinnamon**
¾ **cup freshly ground coffee**
8 **whole allspice**
8 **whole cloves**
Honey (optional)

Place cold water and cinnamon sticks in the bottom of an electric percolator. Place coffee, allspice, and cloves in the percolator basket. Perk through the complete cycle of electric percolator. Serve Spiced Coffee hot, and sweeten it with honey, if desired. Yield: 6 cups.

SPANISH CREAM COFFEE

½ **cup freshly ground coffee**
4 **cups water**
1 **cup sugar**
1 **cup boiling water**
1 **cup half-and-half**
1 **pint vanilla ice cream**

Brew coffee and 4 cups water as desired to make strong coffee.

Cook sugar over medium-high heat in a heavy skillet, stirring constantly, until sugar melts and forms a light brown syrup. Reduce heat to low; gradually add boiling water in a slow stream, stirring constantly. Bring mixture to a boil, and boil 2 minutes. Add the brewed coffee and half-and-half. Serve over ice in tall glasses; top each serving with a small scoop of ice cream. Yield: 6 servings.

Cookies and Candies

LEMON WHIPPERSNAPS

1 (18¼-ounce) package lemon cake
    mix with pudding
2 cups frozen whipped topping,
    thawed
1 egg, slightly beaten
1 teaspoon grated lemon rind
½ cup sifted powdered sugar

Combine first 4 ingredients in a large mixing bowl; stir until well blended. Drop by teaspoonfuls into powdered sugar; roll until coated. Place 1½ inches apart on lightly greased cookie sheets. Bake at 350° for 10 to 12 minutes. Remove the cookies immediately, and cool them on wire racks. Yield: about 5 dozen.

SHORTBREAD TOFFEE SQUARES

1 cup all-purpose flour
¼ cup sifted powdered sugar
½ cup butter or margarine, melted
1 (14-ounce) can sweetened
    condensed milk
2 tablespoons sugar
¼ cup butter or margarine
½ teaspoon vanilla extract
1 (4-ounce) package sweet baking
    chocolate
2 tablespoons water
½ cup chopped pecans

Combine flour and powdered sugar; add ½ cup melted butter, mixing well. Press mixture into a 9-inch square pan. Bake at 350° for 18 to 20 minutes or until lightly browned.

Combine sweetened condensed milk, sugar, and ¼ cup butter in a heavy saucepan; cook over medium heat, stirring constantly, until mixture leaves sides of pan. Stir in vanilla. Pour over crust; cool.

Even Scrooge would find something he liked here. This assortment of cookies and candies features (front to back) Sweet Potato Candy, Shortbread Toffee Squares, Lemon Whippersnaps, Brownie Drops, Citrus-Raisin Cookies, Twice-Cooked Divinity, and Orange Candy.

Combine chocolate and water in top of a double boiler; bring water to a boil. Reduce heat to low; cook until chocolate melts, stirring occasionally. Spread chocolate over toffee mixture; sprinkle with pecans. Cut into squares. Yield: 3 dozen.

CITRUS-RAISIN COOKIES

       1 cup butter or margarine, softened
       1 cup sugar
       1 cup firmly packed brown sugar
       2 eggs, slightly beaten
       1 teaspoon vanilla extract
    2¼ cups all-purpose flour
       1 teaspoon baking powder
     ½ teaspoon baking soda
     ¼ teaspoon salt
       1 cup flaked coconut
    1½ cups regular oats, uncooked
       1 cup chopped pecans
       2 cups raisins
       1 teaspoon grated orange rind
       1 teaspoon grated lemon rind

Cream butter in a large mixing bowl; gradually add sugars, beating well. Add eggs and vanilla; beat well. Combine flour and next 3 ingredients; add to the creamed mixture, mixing until blended. Stir in the remaining ingredients.

Drop dough by teaspoonfuls onto lightly greased cookie sheets. Bake at 375° for 10 to 12 minutes. Cool cookies on wire racks. Yield: 7 dozen.

ROLLED CHRISTMAS COOKIES

       1 cup butter or margarine, softened
       1 cup sugar
       2 eggs
     ¼ cup milk
    1½ teaspoons vanilla extract
       3 cups all-purpose flour
       2 teaspoons baking powder
     ¾ teaspoon baking soda
     ¼ teaspoon ground cardamom
         Royal Icing
         Assorted candies (optional)

Cream butter; gradually add sugar, beating at medium speed of an electric mixer until light and fluffy. Add eggs, one at a time, beating after each addition. Add milk and vanilla, and mix well. Combine flour, baking powder, soda, and cardamom; add flour mixture to creamed mixture, stirring until blended.

Shape dough into a ball; wrap in plastic wrap, and chill at least 2 hours.

Roll dough to ⅛-inch thickness on a lightly floured surface; cut with shaped cookie cutters. Place cookies on lightly greased cookie sheets; bake at 375° for 8 minutes or until edges are lightly browned. Cool on wire racks. Decorate with Royal Icing and assorted candies, if desired. Yield: 6 dozen (3-inch) cookies.

Royal Icing:

       3 large egg whites
     ½ teaspoon cream of tartar
       1 (16-ounce) package powdered
           sugar, sifted
         Paste food coloring

Combine egg whites and cream of tartar in a large mixing bowl. Beat at medium speed of an electric mixer until frothy. Gradually add powdered sugar, mixing well; beat mixture at high speed 5 to 7 minutes. Tint as desired with paste food coloring. Yield: about 2 cups.

Note: Icing dries very quickly; keep covered at all times with plastic wrap.

PECAN MILLIONAIRES

       3 cups pecan halves
       1 (14-ounce) package caramels
       4 (2-ounce) squares chocolate
           almond bark

Arrange pecan halves in groups of 5 on lightly greased cookie sheets, each group resembling head and legs of a turtle. Place an unwrapped caramel in the center of each pecan cluster. Bake at 325° for 8 to 10 minutes or until caramel melts. Lift with greased spatula onto wire rack to cool.

Place almond bark in the top of a double boiler, and bring the water to a boil. Reduce heat to low; cook until almond bark melts, stirring occasionally. Spread on top of turtles. Yield: 4 dozen.

CHOCOLATE-PRALINE JUMBO CHRISTMAS MUD SQUARES

¾ cup graham cracker crumbs
¾ cup finely chopped pecans
¼ cup firmly packed brown sugar
¼ cup butter or margarine,
    melted
1 (12-ounce) jar commercial caramel
    flavored topping
3 tablespoons all-purpose flour
1 cup butter or margarine
4 (1-ounce) squares unsweetened
    chocolate
1½ cups sugar
1 cup all-purpose flour
4 eggs, beaten
1 teaspoon vanilla extract
    Chocolate frosting (recipe follows)
    Pecan halves (optional)
    Candied cherries (optional)

Combine graham cracker crumbs, pecans, brown sugar, and butter, stirring well. Press the crumb mixture into the bottom of a greased 9-inch square pan. Bake at 350° for 8 to 10 minutes, and cool slightly.

Combine caramel topping and 3 tablespoons flour, stirring well. Spread topping on crust to within ¼ inch from edge of pan. Set aside.

Combine 1 cup butter and unsweetened chocolate in a heavy saucepan; cook over low heat until melted. Stir in sugar and next 3 ingredients; pour mixture over caramel topping. Bake at 350° for 50 minutes. Cool

slightly and spread with chocolate frosting. Garnish with pecan halves and candied cherries, if desired. Yield: 16 squares.

Chocolate Frosting:

1 tablespoon butter or margarine
2 tablespoons cocoa
2 tablespoons water
1 cup sifted powdered sugar
¼ teaspoon vanilla extract

Combine first 3 ingredients in a small saucepan; cook over medium heat until mixture thickens. Remove from heat; stir in the powdered sugar and vanilla. Yield: about 1 cup.

BROWNIE DROPS

2 (4-ounce) packages sweet baking
    chocolate
1 tablespoon butter
2 eggs
¾ cup sugar
¼ cup all-purpose flour
¼ teaspoon baking powder
⅛ teaspoon salt
¼ teaspoon ground cinnamon
½ teaspoon vanilla extract
    Walnut halves

Combine chocolate and butter in top of a double boiler; bring water to a boil. Reduce heat to low; cook until chocolate melts, stirring occasionally. Cool, and set aside.

Beat eggs at high speed of an electric mixer until foamy. Gradually add sugar, 1 tablespoon at a time, beating until mixture is thick and lemon colored (about 5 minutes). Add chocolate mixture and next 4 ingredients, mixing well. Stir in vanilla. Drop by teaspoonfuls 3 inches apart on greased cookie sheets. Press a walnut half into center of each cookie. Bake at 350° for 8 to 10 minutes. Cool on wire rack. Yield: 5 dozen.

ORANGE CANDY

    1 **thick-skinned orange**
1¾ **cups sugar**
    1 **cup evaporated milk**
    8 **marshmallows, quartered**
    2 **cups pecan halves**

Peel orange, reserving orange sections for other uses. Place orange peel in a medium saucepan; cover with water and cook 15 minutes or until tender. Remove white membrane from peel and discard. Cut peel into ⅛-inch strips. Cut strips into 1-inch lengths; set aside.

Combine sugar and milk in a large heavy saucepan; bring to a boil. Cover and boil 3 minutes. Uncover and cook, stirring constantly, until mixture reaches 220°. Remove from heat; add marshmallows, stirring until melted. Beat until creamy. Stir in pecans and orange peel. Working rapidly, drop by rounded teaspoonfuls onto waxed paper; cool. Yield: about 4 dozen.

TWICE-COOKED DIVINITY

    2 **cups sugar**
½ **cup water**
½ **cup light corn syrup**
    Dash of salt
    2 **egg whites**
    1 **teaspoon vanilla extract**
    Candied cherries, halved (optional)

Combine sugar, water, corn syrup, and salt in a heavy saucepan; cook mixture over medium heat, stirring constantly, until sugar dissolves. Bring to a boil; cover and cook 3 minutes. Uncover and cook over high heat, without stirring, until mixture reaches soft ball stage (240°).

Beat egg whites (at room temperature) in a large mixing bowl until stiff peaks form.

With goodies like these, kids will pack gift tins using the "two for it, one for me" method, so plan to cook extras.

Pour one-third of hot sugar mixture in a very thin stream over egg whites, while beating constantly at high speed of an electric mixer.

Cook remaining syrup, without stirring, until mixture reaches hard ball stage (265°). Pour remaining hot syrup in a very thin stream over egg white mixture, while beating constantly at high speed of an electric mixer. Add vanilla, and continue beating 3 to 4 minutes, until mixture holds its shape.

Quickly drop mixture by heaping teaspoonfuls onto waxed paper. Garnish with candied cherry halves, if desired. Cool. Yield: 2 dozen.

SWEET POTATO CANDY

     1 cup hot mashed sweet potato
    ¼ cup butter or margarine
     2 (1-pound) packages plus 1 cup
        sifted powdered sugar
     1 teaspoon vanilla extract
    12 (1-ounce) squares unsweetened
        chocolate
     1 tablespoon shortening
        Chopped pecans (optional)

Combine mashed sweet potato and butter in large mixing bowl; beat well with an electric mixer. Gradually add sugar, beating well after each addition, until mixture is firm enough to shape. Stir in vanilla. Shape into 1-inch balls; chill.

Combine chocolate and shortening in top of a double boiler; bring water to a boil. Reduce heat to low; cook until chocolate melts, stirring occasionally. Dip each ball into chocolate. Sprinkle with chopped pecans, if desired. Place on waxed paper; chill until firm. Store in an airtight container in refrigerator. Yield: about 6 dozen.

Note: Nine (2-ounce) squares chocolate almond bark may be substituted for chocolate and shortening.

HEAVENLY CARAMELS

    12 double graham crackers
     2 cups miniature marshmallows
    ¾ cup butter or margarine
    ¾ cup firmly packed brown sugar
     1 teaspoon ground cinnamon
     1 teaspoon vanilla extract
     1 cup sliced almonds
     1 cup flaked coconut

Arrange crackers in a greased 15- x 10- x 1-inch jellyroll pan. Sprinkle with marshmallows; set aside.

Combine butter, brown sugar, and cinnamon in a heavy saucepan; cook over medium heat, stirring constantly, until sugar dissolves. Remove from heat; stir in vanilla. Spoon mixture over marshmallows. Sprinkle with almonds and coconut. Bake at 350° for 12 to 14 minutes. Cool in pan on a wire rack. Cut into 24 squares, and cut each square in half to form a triangle. Yield: 4 dozen.

SOUR CREAM FUDGE

     2 cups sugar
    ¾ cup commercial sour cream
    ¼ cup milk
     2 tablespoons light corn syrup
     2 tablespoons butter
     1 teaspoon vanilla extract
    ½ cup chopped walnuts

Combine first 5 ingredients in a heavy saucepan; bring to a boil. Cover and cook 3 minutes. Uncover and cook, without stirring, until mixture reaches 230°. Remove from heat, and let stand 15 minutes.

Add vanilla and walnuts; beat with a wooden spoon until mixture thickens and begins to lose its gloss (2 to 3 minutes). Pour into a buttered 8-inch square dish. Cool and cut into squares. Yield: 3 dozen.

Cakes and Pies

BLACK FOREST PIE

¾ cup sugar
⅓ cup cocoa
2 tablespoons all-purpose flour
¼ cup butter or margarine
⅓ cup milk
2 eggs, beaten
1 (21-ounce) can cherry pie filling, divided
1 unbaked (9-inch) pastry shell
1 cup whipping cream
1½ tablespoons powdered sugar
Grated chocolate

Combine first 3 ingredients in a saucepan; blend well. Add butter and milk. Cook over medium heat, stirring constantly, until mixture boils and thickens. Remove from heat. Gradually stir about one-fourth of hot mixture into beaten eggs; add to remaining hot mixture, stirring constantly. Cook over medium-low heat, stirring constantly, for 2 minutes. Remove from heat. Stir in about half of cherry pie filling. Pour mixture into pastry shell. Bake at 350° for 35 minutes or until center is set but still shiny. Cool completely on a wire rack. Chill 1 hour.

Combine whipping cream and powdered sugar; beat at medium speed of an electric mixer until stiff peaks form. Garnish outside edge with whipped cream, and sprinkle with grated chocolate. Spoon remaining pie filling in center of pie. Chill. Yield: one 9-inch pie.

CRANBERRY TART

3 cups fresh cranberries
⅔ cup red currant jelly
1 cup sugar
1 tablespoon grated orange rind
½ cup water
¼ cup cornstarch
1½ tablespoons Grand Marnier
Tart shell (recipe follows)
Sweetened whipped cream
Orange rind (optional)

Combine first 6 ingredients in a medium saucepan. Cook over low heat until berries are soft (not bursting) and mixture thickens. Remove from heat; stir in Grand Marnier, and let cool. Pour into baked tart shell. Garnish with whipped cream and orange rind, if desired. Yield: 9 to 12 servings.

Tart Shell:

1½ cups all-purpose flour
2 tablespoons brown sugar
½ cup butter or margarine
1 egg yolk
5 to 7 tablespoons cold water

Combine flour and sugar; cut in butter with pastry blender until mixture resembles coarse meal. Stir in egg yolk. Sprinkle water evenly over surface, 1 tablespoon at a time; stir with a fork until dry ingredients are moistened. Shape into a ball; chill.

Roll dough to ⅛-inch thickness on a lightly floured surface. Fit pastry into a 12- x 8- x 1- inch tart pan. Prick bottom of pastry with a fork. Bake at 450° for 10 to 12 minutes or until golden brown. Cool. Yield: 1 tart shell.

Garnish Black Forest Pie with whipped cream and grated chocolate for a dessert that tastes as good as it looks.

VANILLA CREAM PIE
WITH BLUEBERRY SAUCE

⅓ cup sugar
1 envelope unflavored gelatin
¼ teaspoon salt
3 eggs, separated
1½ cups milk
1 teaspoon vanilla extract
¼ cup sugar
½ cup whipping cream
1 baked 9-inch pastry shell
1 cup commercial blueberry sauce

Combine first 3 ingredients in top of a double boiler; stir in egg yolks and milk. Bring water to a boil; reduce heat to low, and cook, stirring constantly, about 10 minutes or until thickened. Remove from heat; stir in vanilla, and let cool. Chill until consistency of unbeaten egg white.

Beat egg whites (at room temperature) at high speed of an electric mixer 1 minute. Gradually add sugar, beating until stiff peaks form; fold into gelatin mixture. Beat whipping cream until stiff peaks form; fold into gelatin mixture. Pour into pastry shell; chill at least 4 hours. Serve with blueberry sauce. Yield: one 9-inch pie.

LADY BALTIMORE CAKE

1 cup butter or margarine, softened
2 cups sugar, divided
3½ cups sifted cake flour
1 tablespoon baking powder
½ teaspoon salt
1 cup milk
2 teaspoons vanilla extract
7 egg whites
Lady Baltimore Filling
Seven-Minute Frosting
Candied red cherries, sliced

Cream butter; gradually add 1¾ cups sugar, beating at medium speed of an electric mixer, until light and fluffy.

Complete a holiday dinner with an enticing slice of Lady Baltimore Cake.

Combine flour, baking powder, and salt; add to creamed mixture alternately with milk, beginning and ending with flour mixture. Mix well after each addition. Stir in vanilla. Beat egg whites (at room temperature) at high speed of an electric mixer until foamy. Gradually add remaining sugar, beating until stiff peaks form; fold into batter.

Pour batter into 3 greased and floured 9-inch round cakepans. Bake at 350° for 20 to 25 minutes or until a wooden pick inserted in center comes out clean. Cool in pans 10 minutes; remove from pans, and cool completely on wire racks.

Spread Lady Baltimore Filling between layers; frost top and sides with Seven-Minute Frosting. Garnish with candied cherries. Yield: one 3-layer cake.

Lady Baltimore Filling:

1 cup chopped pecans
¾ cup chopped dates
½ cup chopped candied red cherries
½ cup golden raisins
¼ cup bourbon

Combine all ingredients in a bowl; let stand 1 hour. Fold in about 2 cups of Seven-Minute Frosting. Yield: 4½ cups.

Seven-Minute Frosting:

2¼ cups sugar
3 egg whites
1½ tablespoons light corn syrup
    Dash of salt
½ cup water
1½ teaspoons vanilla extract

Combine first 5 ingredients in top of a large double boiler. Beat at low speed of an electric mixer 30 seconds or until just blended.

Place over boiling water; beat constantly on high speed 7 minutes or until stiff peaks form. Remove from heat. Add vanilla; beat 2 minutes or until frosting is thick enough to spread. Yield: 7 cups.

CHOCOLATE PECAN TORTE

4 eggs, separated
½ cup sugar
¾ cup ground pecans
⅓ cup all-purpose flour
⅓ cup cocoa
½ teaspoon baking soda
¼ teaspoon salt
¼ cup water
1 teaspoon vanilla extract
¼ cup sugar
    Chocolate frosting (recipe follows)
¾ cup chopped pecans
    Chocolate glaze (recipe follows)
    Chocolate leaves (optional)

Grease bottoms of two 9-inch round cake-pans, line with waxed paper, and grease paper.

Beat egg yolks at high speed of an electric mixer until foamy. Gradually add ½ cup sugar, beating until mixture is thick and lemon colored.

Combine ground pecans, flour, cocoa, soda, and salt; add to yolk mixture alternately with water, beginning and ending with pecan mixture. Stir in vanilla.

Beat egg whites (at room temperature) at high speed of an electric mixer until foamy. Gradually add ¼ cup sugar, beating until stiff peaks form; fold into pecan mixture. Spread batter in prepared pans. Bake at 375° for 16 to 18 minutes. Cool in pans 10 minutes; remove layers from pans. Remove waxed paper; cool completely on wire racks.

Split cake layers in half horizontally to make 4 layers. Place 1 cake layer on serving plate; spread with 1 cup chocolate frosting. Repeat procedure with second and third cake layers, and top with fourth cake layer. Frost sides of cake with chocolate frosting and pat ¾ cup chopped pecans on frosting around sides of cake. Spread chocolate glaze over top of cake. Garnish with chocolate leaves, if desired. Yield: one 9-inch cake.

Chocolate Frosting:

½ cup plus 2 tablespoons sifted
    powdered sugar
¼ cup plus 1 tablespoon cocoa
2 cups whipping cream
1½ teaspoons vanilla extract

Combine powdered sugar and cocoa; gradually add whipping cream. Beat at low speed of an electric mixer until blended; beat at high speed until stiff peaks form. Stir in vanilla. Yield: about 4 cups.

Chocolate Glaze:

1 tablespoon butter or margarine
2 tablespoons cocoa
2 tablespoons water
1 cup sifted powdered sugar
¼ teaspoon vanilla extract

Combine butter, cocoa, and water in a small saucepan; cook over medium heat until mixture thickens, stirring constantly. Remove from heat. Stir in powdered sugar and vanilla, blending well. Add additional water, if needed, for desired spreading consistency. Yield: about 1 cup.

HOLIDAY CAKE

1 (18.5-ounce) package white cake
    mix with pudding
1¼ cups water
⅓ cup vegetable oil
3 egg whites
    Cherry-Amaretto Topping
    Chocolate frosting (recipe follows)
    Sweetened whipped cream
    (optional)

Combine cake mix, water, vegetable oil, and egg whites in a large mixing bowl; beat 2 minutes at medium speed of an electric mixer. Pour batter into 3 greased and floured 9-inch round cakepans. Bake at 350° for 20 minutes or until a wooden pick inserted in the center comes out clean. Cool the cakes in pans 10 minutes; remove cakes from the pans, and let them cool completely on wire racks.

Spread half of Cherry-Amaretto Topping on 1 cake layer; top with second cake layer, and spread with one-third of chocolate frosting. Top with third cake layer, and spread with remaining Cherry-Amaretto Topping. Spread remaining chocolate frosting on sides of cake. Garnish with whipped cream, if desired. Yield: one 3-layer cake.

Cherry-Amaretto Topping:

2 (16-ounce) jars red maraschino
    cherries
¼ cup plus 1 teaspoon cornstarch
3 tablespoons sugar
⅓ cup amaretto

Drain cherries and reserve 1 cup juice. Quarter cherries and set aside 2 cups, reserving remaining cherries and juice for other uses. Combine cornstarch and sugar in a small saucepan; stir in 1 cup cherry juice and amaretto. Cook over medium heat, stirring constantly, until mixture thickens. Remove from heat, and stir in cherries. Cool. Yield: 2 cups.

Chocolate Frosting:

3 (1-ounce) squares unsweetened
    chocolate
¼ cup butter or margarine,
    softened
4 cups sifted powdered sugar
½ cup milk
1½ teaspoons vanilla extract
½ cup chopped pecans, toasted

Place chocolate in top of a double boiler; bring water to a boil. Reduce heat to low; cook until chocolate melts.

Cream butter with an electric mixer; add melted chocolate, powdered sugar, and milk, beating until mixture is smooth. Stir in vanilla and pecans. Yield: 3 cups.

CARAMEL-PECAN PIE

1 cup coarsely chopped pecans
1 unbaked 9-inch pastry shell
¼ cup commercial caramel topping
2 (3-ounce) packages cream cheese,
    softened
½ cup sugar
1 teaspoon vanilla extract
3 eggs
    Pecan halves (optional)
    Commercial caramel topping
    (optional)

Place 1 cup pecans in bottom of pastry shell; drizzle with ¼ cup caramel topping. Set aside.

Combine cream cheese, sugar, and vanilla; beat at medium speed of an electric mixer until well blended. Add eggs, one at a time, beating after each addition. Pour mixture over pecans. Bake at 325° for 45 minutes. Cool completely, and chill. Garnish with pecan halves and drizzle with additional caramel topping, if desired. Yield: one 9-inch pie.

Party Fare

CHICKEN BITS À L'ORANGE

¼ cup plus 1 tablespoon all-purpose
   flour
1 teaspoon chili powder
1 teaspoon salt
4 chicken breast halves, skinned,
   boned, and cut into bite-size
   pieces
½ cup butter or margarine, melted
2 tablespoons brown sugar
1½ tablespoons grated orange rind
1 teaspoon ground ginger
½ teaspoon dried whole rosemary
2 cups orange juice
¼ cup Cointreau or other orange
   flavored liqueur
   Orange slices (optional)
   Parsley (optional)

Combine flour, chili powder, and salt;
dredge chicken with flour mixture, reserving
leftover flour mixture.

Brown chicken in butter in a large skillet.
Remove chicken, reserving pan drippings;
drain, and set aside. Add reserved flour mixture, brown sugar, orange rind, ginger, and
rosemary to drippings in skillet, stirring
until smooth. Cook over medium heat, stirring constantly, 1 minute. Gradually add
orange juice and Cointreau, and cook until
thickened and bubbly. Add chicken, reduce
heat, and simmer about 30 minutes or until
tender, stirring frequently.

Serve in chafing dish. Garnish with orange
slices and parsley, if desired. Yield: 8 appetizer servings.

*For stylish holiday entertaining, begin with a
spread of delectable appetizers. From front,
Marinated Vegetables, Vegetable-Stuffed
Mushrooms, Shrimp Remoulade,
Walnut-Roquefort Cheese, and Chicken Bits à
l'Orange.*

WALNUT-ROQUEFORT CHEESE

1 envelope unflavored gelatin
½ cup water
1 (8-ounce) package cream cheese, softened
1½ ounces Roquefort cheese
¼ teaspoon salt
1 cup whipping cream
½ cup finely chopped walnuts

Sprinkle gelatin over water in a saucepan; let stand 5 minutes. Place over medium heat, stirring until gelatin dissolves.

Combine cream cheese, Roquefort cheese, and salt in a mixing bowl; beat at medium speed of an electric mixer until creamy and smooth. Add gelatin; beat well. Add whipping cream, beating until fluffy.

Sprinkle walnuts in bottom of a lightly oiled 4-cup mold; pour in cheese mixture. Chill until firm. Unmold onto serving plate. Serve with fruit or crackers. Yield: 4 cups.

ORIENTAL CRAB APPETIZERS

½ cup chopped green onions
3 tablespoons butter or margarine, melted
2 (8-ounce) packages cream cheese, cubed
2 (6-ounce) cans crabmeat, drained and flaked
¼ cup half-and-half
½ teaspoon Chinese five-spice seasoning
⅛ teaspoon garlic powder
4½ dozen wonton skins
Vegetable oil
1 (9-ounce) bottle commercial sweet-and-sour sauce

Sauté green onions in butter; add cream cheese, crabmeat, half-and-half, and seasonings. Cook over low heat, stirring, until

cream cheese melts. Remove from heat. Place 1 tablespoon crab mixture in center of each wonton. Moisten edges. Fold in half diagonally. Seal edges. Bend ends of folded edge together.

Heat 1 inch oil to 375° in a wok or large skillet. Place several wontons at a time in hot oil, and fry 30 seconds on each side; drain on paper towels. Repeat with remaining wontons. Serve with sweet-and-sour sauce. Yield: about 4½ dozen.

SHRIMP REMOULADE

1 egg
2 tablespoons paprika
1 teaspoon salt
¼ cup plus 2 tablespoons creole mustard
¼ cup catsup
1½ cups vegetable oil
¼ cup white wine vinegar
1 clove garlic, minced
1 tablespoon prepared horseradish
¼ teaspoon ground bay leaves
¼ cup chopped onion
¼ cup chopped celery
¼ cup chopped parsley
¼ teaspoon hot sauce
1 lemon, cut into wedges
4½ quarts water
6 pounds unpeeled shrimp
Lettuce leaves

Combine first 5 ingredients in mixing bowl; beat well. Add oil in a slow steady stream, beating at medium speed of an electric mixer until mixture is thick. Add vinegar and next 7 ingredients. Squeeze juice from lemon wedges into mixture; add lemon wedges, and stir well. Cover and refrigerate.

Bring water to a boil; add shrimp, and cook 3 to 5 minutes. Drain well; rinse with cold water. Chill. Peel and devein shrimp.

Pour sauce over shrimp; stir well. Cover and chill 8 hours. Serve in a lettuce-lined bowl. Yield: 50 appetizer servings.

DEVILED HAM LOAF

2 (4¼-ounce) cans deviled ham
1 (8-ounce) package cream cheese, softened
2 tablespoons minced onion
¼ cup sweet pickle relish
⅛ teaspoon Worcestershire sauce
1 cup commercial sour dressing
   Sliced pimiento-stuffed olives (optional)

Combine all ingredients except sour dressing and olives; mix well. Shape into a loaf; chill 1 hour. Frost with sour dressing, and garnish with olives, if desired. Serve on assorted party breads or crackers. Yield: about 3 cups.

Certain to be crowd pleasers, Vegetable-Stuffed Mushrooms and Walnut-Roquefort Cheese will satisfy the eye as well as the palate. A mold gives fluted edges to the walnut-cheese mixture, while parsley and radish slices embellish the tops of the mushrooms.

MARINATED VEGETABLES

1 (0.7-ounce) package Italian salad dressing mix
½ cup olive oil
½ cup white wine vinegar
½ pound small fresh green beans
2 carrots, scraped and sliced diagonally
1 turnip, thinly sliced
1 sweet red pepper, cut into 2-inch strips
1 (8-ounce) package white radishes, cut into 2-inch strips
   Leaf lettuce

Combine first 3 ingredients in a jar; cover tightly, and shake vigorously until well blended. Set aside.

Cut beans into 2-inch pieces; cook in a small amount of boiling water until beans are crisp-tender. Place beans and remaining vegetables in a 13- x 9- x 2-inch dish. (Do not combine vegetables.) Pour marinade over them. Cover and chill 8 hours.

Drain, and arrange on lettuce-lined serving platter. Yield: 10 to 12 servings.

VEGETABLE-STUFFED MUSHROOMS

36 medium-size fresh mushrooms
2 (3-ounce) packages cream cheese, softened
⅓ cup commercial sour cream
¼ cup minced radishes
¼ cup minced celery
¼ cup minced fresh parsley
2 tablespoons minced onion
1 teaspoon lemon juice
¼ teaspoon salt
¼ teaspoon white pepper
   Sliced radishes (optional)
   Parsley sprigs (optional)

Clean the mushrooms with damp paper towels. Remove the mushroom stems, and reserve them for other uses; set caps aside until ready to use.

Combine cream cheese and sour cream in a small bowl; beat at medium speed of an electric mixer until smooth. Stir in the minced radishes and the next 6 ingredients; blend well. Spoon the mixture into mushroom caps. Garnish with radish slices and parsley, if desired. Chill. Yield: 36 stuffed mushrooms.

MUSHROOM TARTS

¾ **cup chopped onion**
2 **tablespoons butter or margarine, melted**
1 **pound fresh mushrooms, chopped**
1 **tablespoon lemon juice**
½ **teaspoon salt**
  Pinch of pepper
1 **tablespoon cornstarch**
1 **tablespoon water**
1 **cup whipping cream**
  Tart shells (recipe follows)
¼ **cup (1 ounce) shredded Gruyère cheese**

Sauté onion in butter in a large skillet until tender. Stir in mushrooms; cook until liquid evaporates (about 10 minutes). Stir in lemon juice, salt, and pepper.

Combine cornstarch and water in a saucepan; stir in whipping cream. Cook over low heat, stirring constantly, until thick and bubbly. Stir sauce into mushroom mixture.

Fill baked tart shells with 1 tablespoon filling; sprinkle with cheese. Place on ungreased cookie sheets, and bake at 400° for 10 minutes or until cheese melts. Yield: 3 dozen.

Tart Shells:

2 **cups all-purpose flour**
1 **teaspoon salt**
¾ **cup butter or margarine**
¼ **cup cold water**

Combine flour and salt; cut in butter with pastry blender until mixture resembles coarse meal. Sprinkle water, 1 tablespoon at a time, evenly over surface; stir with a fork until dry ingredients are moistened. Shape dough into a ball, and chill.

Divide dough into 36 balls. Place balls in individual wells of ungreased 1¾-inch muffin pans, pressing dough onto bottom and sides to form shells. Bake at 425° for 10 minutes or until lightly browned. Remove to wire rack. Let cool 5 minutes. Yield: 3 dozen shells.

Note: Mushroom Tarts may be frozen before adding cheese. Bake frozen tarts at 400° for 10 minutes. Top with cheese; bake an additional 5 minutes.

OLIVE-NUT BREAD

2½ **cups all-purpose flour**
1 **tablespoon baking powder**
⅓ **cup sugar**
1 **cup pimiento-stuffed olives, sliced**
1 **cup chopped walnuts**
1 **(2-ounce) jar diced pimiento, drained**
1 **egg, beaten**
1¼ **cups milk**
  Cream cheese

Combine flour, baking powder, and sugar; stir well. Add olives, walnuts, and pimiento; stir until well coated. Combine egg and milk, and stir into olive mixture. Spoon batter into 6 greased and floured 4- x 2- x 2-inch loaf-pans; bake at 350° for 25 to 30 minutes or until golden. Serve with cream cheese. Yield: 6 (4- x 2- x 2-inch) loaves.

RIBBON SQUARES

2 **(3½-ounce) packages almond paste**
1½ **cups butter, softened**
1 **cup sugar**
4 **eggs, separated**
1 **teaspoon almond extract**
2 **cups all-purpose flour**
¼ **teaspoon salt**
10 **drops green food coloring**
8 **drops red food coloring**
1 **(12-ounce) jar apricot preserves**
3 **(1-ounce) squares semisweet chocolate**
  Buttercream Frosting

Triple-decked Ribbon Squares are a sweet ending for any meal. Food coloring in the cake batter adds interest to each layer, and Buttercream Frosting tops it all with colorful decorations.

Grease three 15- x 10- x 1-inch jellyroll pans, and line with waxed paper; grease and flour waxed paper; set aside.

Cream almond paste and butter in a large bowl; gradually add sugar, beating at medium speed of an electric mixer until light and fluffy. Add egg yolks, one at a time, beating well after each addition. Add almond extract. Combine flour and salt; add to creamed mixture.

Beat egg whites (at room temperature) at high speed of electric mixer until soft peaks form. Fold egg whites into creamed mixture.

Spread 1½ cups batter evenly in one prepared pan. Add green coloring to 1½ cups batter; mix well, and spread evenly in second prepared pan. Add red coloring to remaining batter; mix well, and spread evenly in remaining prepared pan.

Bake at 350° for 12 minutes or until a wooden pick inserted in center comes out clean. Remove cakes from pans immediately. Peel off waxed paper, and let cool.

Heat apricot preserves in a medium saucepan over low heat; press through a sieve. Place pink cake layer on a cookie sheet; spread with half of preserves. Place yellow layer over preserves. Spread remaining preserves over yellow layer; top with green layer. Cover with plastic wrap. Place a wooden cutting board on entire cake; refrigerate overnight.

Melt chocolate in top of a double boiler. Spread over top of cake. Let stand 30 minutes or until chocolate is set. Trim edges; cut into 1-inch squares. Decorate with Buttercream Frosting. Yield: 88 cakes.

Buttercream Frosting:

   3 **tablespoons butter or margarine, softened**
   2 **cups sifted powdered sugar**
   2 **tablespoons milk**
  ½ **teaspoon vanilla extract**
     Red and green paste coloring

Combine butter; gradually add powdered sugar, beating well. Add milk and vanilla; mix well. Color half of frosting with red food coloring and half with green food coloring. Yield: 1 cup.

Gift Ideas

HOT TACO SAUCE

- 2 quarts peeled and chopped tomatoes
- 1 cup chopped onion
- 1 cup chopped hot peppers
- 1 clove garlic, sliced
- 2½ tablespoons sugar
- 1½ teaspoons dried whole oregano
- ¾ teaspoon salt
- ½ teaspoon ground cloves
- ½ teaspoon ground allspice
- ½ teaspoon ground cinnamon
- ½ teaspoon chili powder
- ½ teaspoon cumin seeds
- ½ teaspoon pickling spice
- ¾ cup vinegar

Combine all ingredients in a Dutch oven. Bring to a boil; reduce heat, and simmer, uncovered, 1 hour. Cool, and store in refrigerator. Yield: 2½ pints.

CHEESE STRAWS

- 4 cups (16 ounces) shredded sharp Cheddar cheese, softened
- ½ cup butter or margarine, softened
- 1¾ cups all-purpose flour
- ½ teaspoon red pepper

Combine cheese and butter in a large mixing bowl; beat at medium speed of an electric mixer until blended. Gradually add flour, mixing until blended. Stir in red pepper. Press dough through a cookie press

Ruffles or ribbon, even a bright red tray— creative packaging and trims enhance the gift appeal of holiday foods. From front, Sweet Nothings, Hot Taco Sauce, and Cheese Straws are ready for delivery.

fitted with a saw-toothed disc, to make long strips lengthwise on ungreased baking sheets. Cut into 2-inch strips. Bake at 350° for 15 to 17 minutes. Remove from baking sheets, and cool on wire racks. Store in an airtight container. Yield: about 7½ dozen.

CURRIED RICE MIX

- 4 cups uncooked long-grain rice
- ¼ cup dried green onion flakes
- 2 tablespoons dried orange rind
- 2 tablespoons plus 2 teaspoons chicken-flavored bouillon granules
- 2 tablespoons dried parsley flakes
- 1 tablespoon plus 1 teaspoon curry powder
- 1 cup mixed dried fruit, chopped
- ½ cup raisins
- 1 cup slivered almonds

Combine all ingredients; stir well. Store in an airtight container. Yield: 7 cups mix.

Recipe for gift card: Bring 2 cups water and 2 tablespoons butter or margarine to a boil in a medium saucepan. Add 1 cup rice mix; cover, reduce heat, and simmer 20 minutes. Yield: about 2½ cups.

HOT CREOLE SEASONING MIX

- ½ cup salt
- ¼ cup plus 1½ tablespoons paprika
- ¼ cup white pepper
- ¼ cup garlic powder
- ¼ cup onion powder
- 3 tablespoons red pepper
- 2 tablespoons dried whole oregano
- 2 tablespoons dried whole thyme
- 1 tablespoon pepper
- 1 teaspoon ground bay leaves

Combine all ingredients in a jar; cover and shake mixture until well blended. Store in an airtight container. Yield: 2 cups.

SWEET NOTHINGS

  3 tablespoons butter or margarine, softened
  2 cups sifted powdered sugar
  2 tablespoons milk
  ½ teaspoon vanilla extract
    Red, green, and yellow paste coloring
  1 (16-ounce) package sugar cubes

Cream butter and powdered sugar with electric mixer until light and fluffy. Add milk and vanilla, beating to spreading consistency. Divide mixture into thirds; color one-third red, one-third green, and one-third yellow. Use No. 66 leaf tip to make holly leaves and No. 2 tip to make holly berries on sugar cubes. (No. 2 tip can also be used to make Christmas trees, stockings, wreaths, and candles.) Yield: 15 dozen.

CHRISTMAS COOKIE WRAP-UP

Basic Cookie Mix:

  4 cups all-purpose flour
1¾ cups sugar
  1 tablespoon baking powder
  1 teaspoon salt
1¼ cups butter-flavored shortening

Combine first four ingredients, mixing well. Cut in shortening with a pastry blender until mixture resembles coarse meal. Store in an airtight container at room temperature up to 3 weeks. Yield: 7 cups.

Chocolate-Mint Drops:

  3 cups Basic Cookie Mix
  ¼ cup cocoa
  2 eggs, beaten
  ¼ cup milk
  1 teaspoon vanilla extract
  ½ cup mint-chocolate morsels
  ½ cup chopped pecans

Combine first 5 ingredients; mix until blended. Stir in chocolate morsels and pecans. Drop by teaspoonfuls onto lightly greased cookie sheets. Bake at 350° for 8 to 10 minutes. Yield: 5 dozen.

Orange-Raisin Cookies:

  3 cups Basic Cookie Mix
  2 eggs, beaten
  ½ cup milk
  2 tablespoons grated orange rind
  1 teaspoon vanilla extract
  ½ teaspoon ground cinnamon
  ½ cup raisins
  ½ cup chopped pecans

Combine first 6 ingredients; mix until blended. Stir in raisins and pecans. Drop by teaspoonfuls onto lightly greased cookie sheets. Bake at 350° for 8 to 10 minutes. Yield: about 5 dozen.

Coconut Squares:

1½ cups Basic Cookie Mix
  1 egg, beaten
  ¼ cup milk
  ½ teaspoon vanilla extract
  ½ cup flaked coconut
  ¼ cup semisweet chocolate morsels
  ¼ cup chopped pecans

Combine first 4 ingredients; mix until blended. Stir in coconut, chocolate morsels, and pecans. Spread mixture into a greased 8-inch square pan. Bake at 350° for 25 to 30 minutes. Cool, and cut into squares. Yield: 2 dozen.

CARDAMOM-CINNAMON SPICE BAGS

    Muslin
24 whole cardamom, cracked
12 (3-inch) cinnamon sticks
    Cotton string

Cut the muslin into twelve 5-inch square pieces. Place 2 cracked cardamom in the center of each square of muslin. Tie securely with cotton string, inserting a cinnamon stick. Yield: 12 bags.

Recipe for gift card: Steep 1 spice bag in ¾ cup hot cranberry juice.

ORANGE-ANISE SPICE BAGS

Muslin
- **3 tablespoons dried orange rind**
- **1 tablespoon plus ½ teaspoon anise seeds**
- **24 whole allspice**
- **Cotton string**

Cut muslin into twelve 5-inch square pieces. Combine orange rind and anise seeds in a small bowl; mix well. Place 1 teaspoon mixture plus 2 whole allspice on each square of muslin. Tie securely with cotton string. Yield: 12 bags.

Recipe for gift card: Steep 1 spice bag in ¾ cup hot apple juice.

SPICED COFFEE MIX

- **1 (2-ounce) jar instant coffee granules**
- **1 cup sugar**
- **1 teaspoon ground allspice**
- **1 teaspoon ground nutmeg**
- **1 teaspoon ground cinnamon**

Combine all ingredients in container of an electric blender; process 15 seconds or until blended. Store in an airtight container. Yield: 2 cups.

Recipe for gift card: Combine 1 to 2 teaspoons mix and ⅔ cup boiling water.

Cardamom-Cinnamon Spice Bags will perk up a cup of hot juice and give friends an excuse to take a break from their holiday rush. A decorative tin keeps the spices pungent and fresh.

Yuletide Tips and Traditions

If there's one message that comes through loud and clear in the letters sent to *Christmas with Southern Living*, it's that there's no end to the ways families revel in all that is Christmas. From the smallest touches to the most unusual twists, a wide array of practices personalizes the holidays for families throughout the South—and probably for yours, too.

This year, we've printed some of the wonderful letters we've received. Enjoy them, pick up some ideas from them, and then jot down your own tips and traditions and send them to us. Our address is *Christmas with Southern Living*, Tips and Traditions, P.O. Box 2262, Birmingham, Alabama 35201.

A Decorating Tip From the Professionals

A trend to watch: companies that offer custom decorating services for Christmas are springing up around the country. They design all manner of decorations for private and corporate clients, install the displays, and store materials between seasons.

One such company, Christmas Designers, in Pompano Beach, Florida, has a tip to share. Minimize damage to outdoor lights by wiring or taping the strands to limbs so they won't be buffeted about by the wind.

A Sampler of Crafters' Traditions

From members of Southern Handcraft Society of Boca Raton, Florida, comes a big batch of tips and traditions:

"My husband and I take our little boy around on Christmas Eve 'looking for Santa.' We look at all the beautiful Christmas decorations for about an hour; then we 'find' Rudolph's nose (a red light on top of a hospital or near an airport) and drive home to see if Santa has delivered his goodies yet."
—Mary Schmidt

"On Christmas Eve, my mother always let us open one gift, which was always a new pair of pajamas (usually either red and white or red, green, and white) so when we got up on Christmas morning, we all had new pj's for the pictures."
—Terri Cowell

"We celebrate two Christmases—a Swedish Christmas on December 13th (St. Lucia Day) and Christmas on December 25th. I wanted my children to remember their Scandinavian heritage, and I make it a Christmas of all homemade crafts that I've made all year long. The children enjoy and look forward to the Swedish more than the traditional Christmas."
—Dot Healy

"When we first moved to Boca Raton 12 years ago, we bought a small fruit tree for Christmas and decorated it instead of a traditional pine tree. After Christmas we planted it in the yard. Now we have three orange trees, two grapefruit trees, a key lime, and an avocado tree."
—Lynne Baldwin

"Any new ornaments for the present year are hung from the chandelier until the Christmas tree is decorated. Our 7½-foot tree holds close to 500 ornaments."
—Joan Booz

"A tradition from my childhood that we've carried over to our children: as we do not have a mantel, Santa fills and hides the stockings. On Christmas morning the children wake up and race around the house looking for their stockings. (A wonderful way to use up some of that Christmas morning energy.) The children may open and enjoy any gifts in the stockings right away, but they may not open the packages under the tree until all of our guests arrive."
—Laura Kluvo

It's a Family Affair

"Christmas is a time of love and sharing for us. For a number of years, after a traditional Thanksgiving dinner for family and friends at my parents' home, we have all converged on Daddy's shop where we have started some project for Christmas. Everybody gets involved—from painting, sawing, nailing, making bows, and offering advice to keeping wood in the stove.

"This year we made 'basket top' door decorations. The day before, Daddy got the basket tops out of the barn where they had been stored for several years and had them in the shop ready for us.

"Daddy's woodpile was the resource for the 'makings' for our reindeer one year. In fact, each year someone wants to add or replace one. And one year the men went to the woods and got a load of grapevines. We made grapevine wreaths, and everyone used their own ideas to decorate them."
　　—Joyce Herron
　　　Ripley, Tennessee

Like a Bowl Full of . . . Butter Beans?

"A small group of us grandmothers are looking forward to our fourth butter bean Christmas party, which takes place a week or two before Christmas. By that time we are tired of decorating, shopping, baking, eating rich foods—we are ready for *plain* old good food, not so fancy and rich.

"The menu always calls for dried lima beans (butter beans, the large kind). In the past we've also had on the menu kraut and wieners, potato salad, fried pork chops, candied yams, cole slaw, sliced onions, and blackberry cobbler.

"We have had place cards with butter beans that have painted Santa faces and a centerpiece with flowers made from butter beans. There are six in our group, and now others have heard what an eating good time we have, and they want to come."
　　—Bobbie Oglesby
　　　Bessemer, Alabama

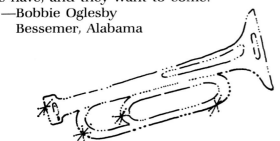

Taking Advantage of Southern Warmth

"We moved to Florida from New England four years ago—our children were six and two years old. When December came, I wondered how we were going to get into the 'Christmas Spirit'—the weather felt more like summer to us! I came up with this idea to start off the month of December.

"On the last day of November my children write their 'Christmas gift list' letters to Santa and address the letters to the North Pole. Before they go to sleep, they put the letters on their windowsills. (The windows are open, of course, letting in the warm Southern night air!) During the night, one of 'Santa's Elves' comes and picks up the letters to bring to Santa—leaving Advent Calendars in their places. So, on the morning of December 1, my children wake up and find their calendars—with one window to open each day until Christmas—and we begin the holiday season!"
　　—Judy Kandzer
　　　Winter Springs, Florida

Creating a Decorating Legacy

"When my children were younger, we would make a special Christmas ornament each year for our tree and to share with friends. When the children grew up and got married, we gave them each a starter box of ornaments with one from each year.

"We now have four grandchildren and two more on the way. A Christmas starter box is being made up for each of them. When we travel during the year we are always on the lookout for a special ornament to add to their box. I plan to make booklets for all of the children, telling them something about the ornaments, such as where and when they were purchased and other information that might be interesting.

"Pleasant memories will brighten many a Christmas, as I hope they will pass our tradition down to future generations."
　　—Marge Gray
　　　Jacksonville, Florida

137

Patterns

Checkers Anyone?

Instructions are on page 82.
Pattern is full-size.

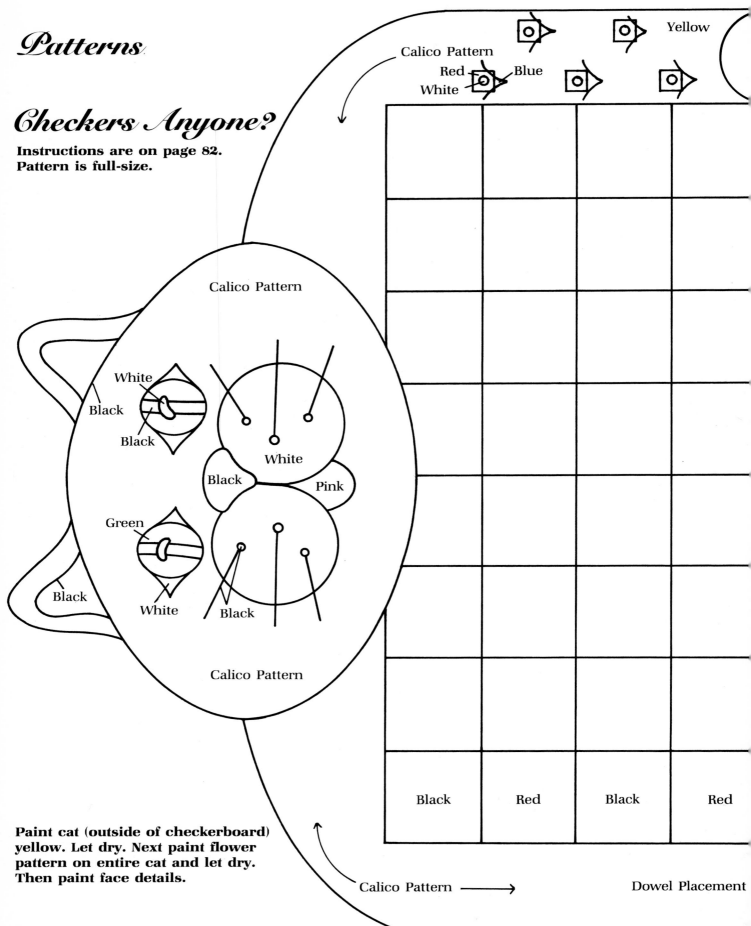

Calico Pattern

Red — Blue
White
Yellow

Calico Pattern

White
Black
Black
White
Black
Pink
Green
Black
White
Black

Calico Pattern

Black	Red	Black	Red

Paint cat (outside of checkerboard) yellow. Let dry. Next paint flower pattern on entire cat and let dry. Then paint face details.

Calico Pattern ⟶   Dowel Placement

Paint sides of board black.

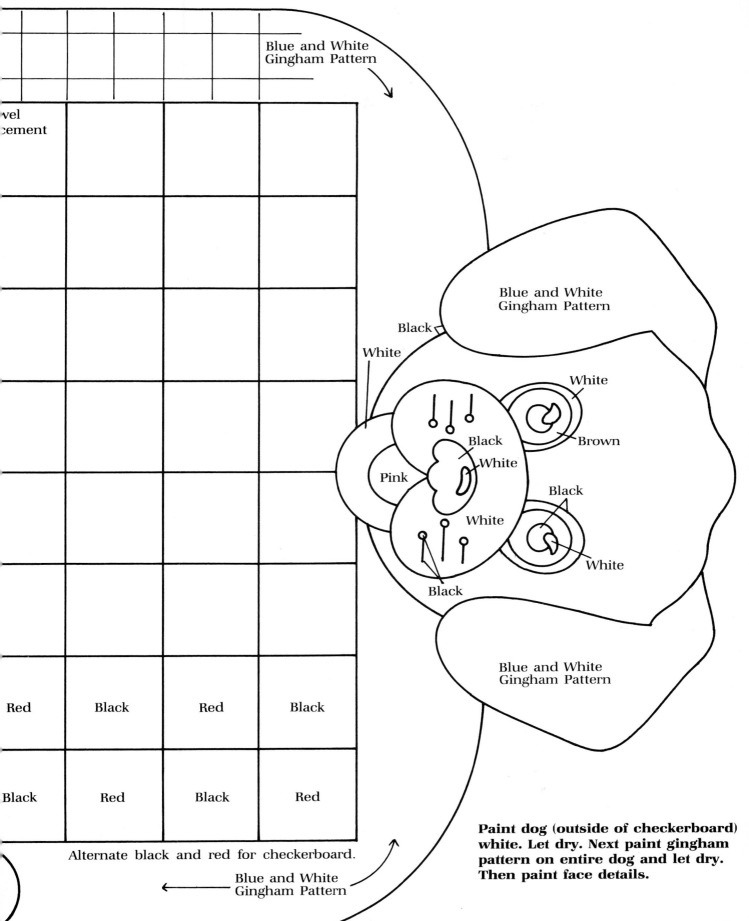

Blue and White Gingham Pattern

vel
cement

Blue and White Gingham Pattern

Black

White

White

Brown

Pink

Black

White

Black

White

White

Black

Black

Red	Black	Red	Black
Black	Red	Black	Red

Alternate black and red for checkerboard.

Blue and White Gingham Pattern

Blue and White Gingham Pattern

Paint dog (outside of checkerboard) white. Let dry. Next paint gingham pattern on entire dog and let dry. Then paint face details.

Paint sides of board black.

Ornaments Galore

Instructions are on page 62.
Patterns are full-size.

Outlines are stitching lines except
for stocking pattern, which includes
¼″ seam allowance. Clip all curves
and angles before turning and stuffing.

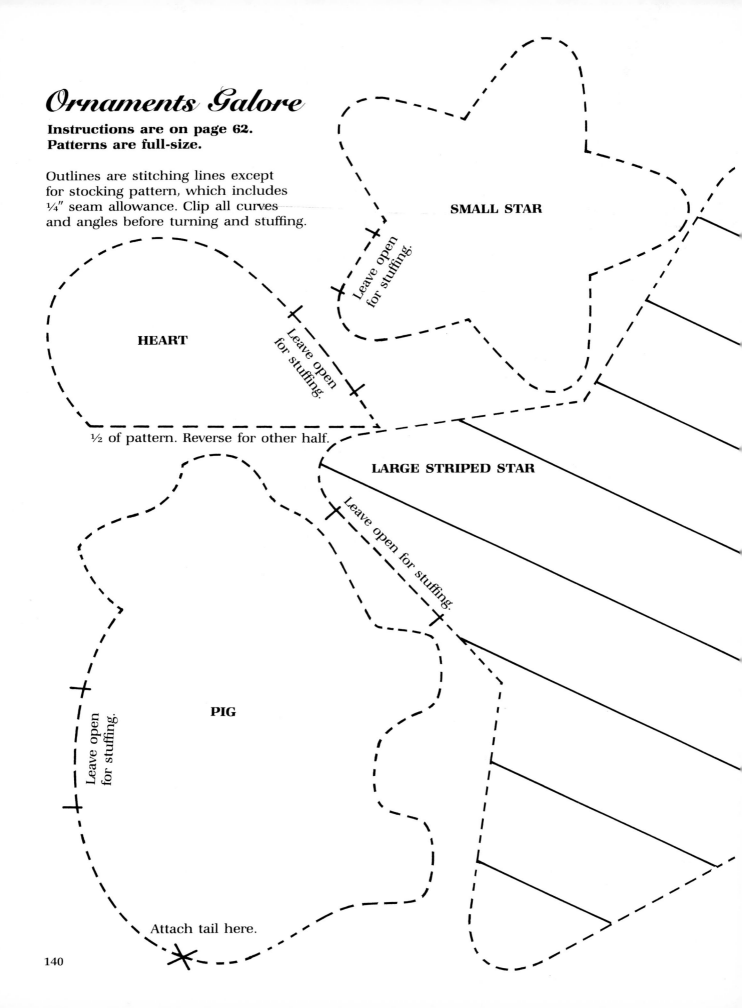

SMALL STAR

Leave open for stuffing.

HEART

Leave open for stuffing.

½ of pattern. Reverse for other half.

LARGE STRIPED STAR

Leave open for stuffing.

Leave open for stuffing.

PIG

Attach tail here.

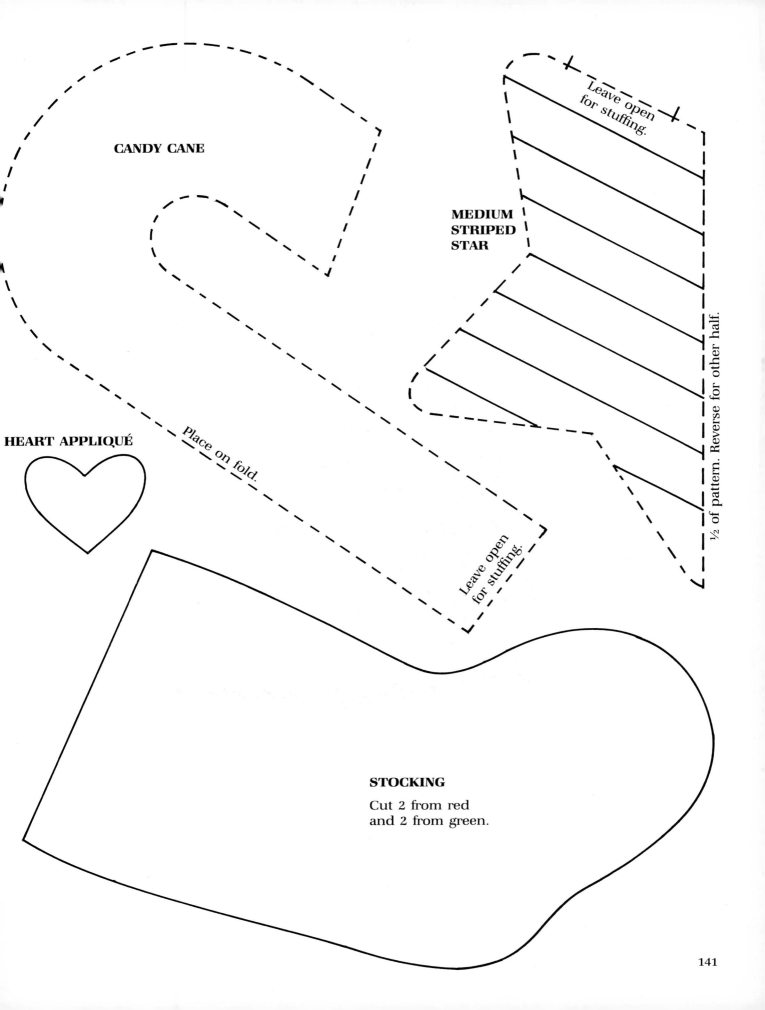

CANDY CANE

MEDIUM STRIPED STAR

Leave open for stuffing.

½ of pattern. Reverse for other half.

HEART APPLIQUÉ

Place on fold.

Leave open for stuffing.

STOCKING

Cut 2 from red
and 2 from green.

141

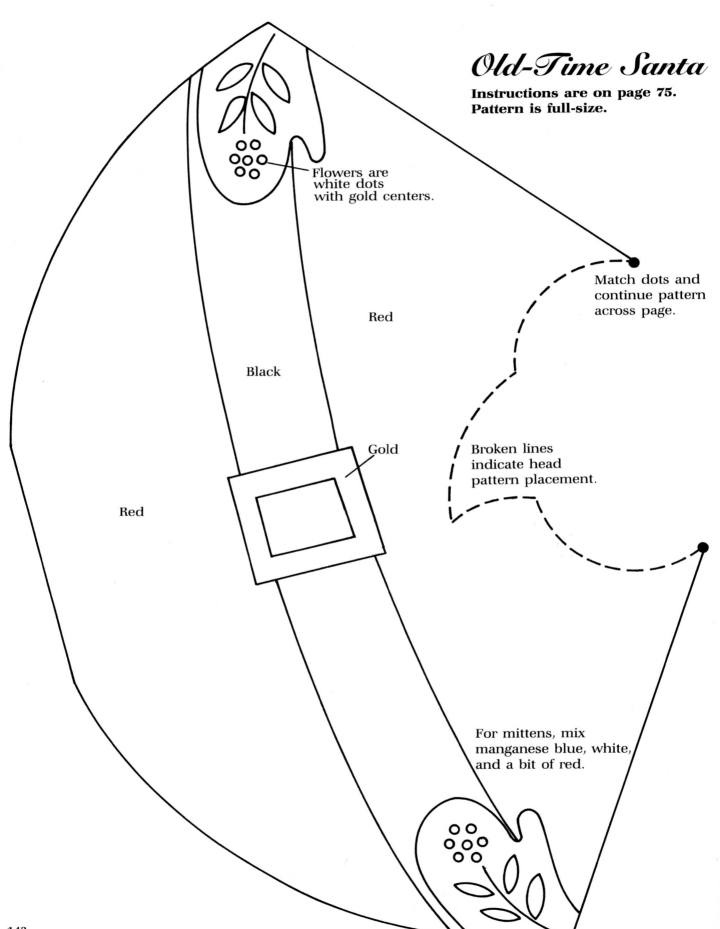

Old-Time Santa

Instructions are on page 75.
Pattern is full-size.

Flowers are white dots with gold centers.

Red

Black

Gold

Red

Match dots and continue pattern across page.

Broken lines indicate head pattern placement.

For mittens, mix manganese blue, white, and a bit of red.

142

142

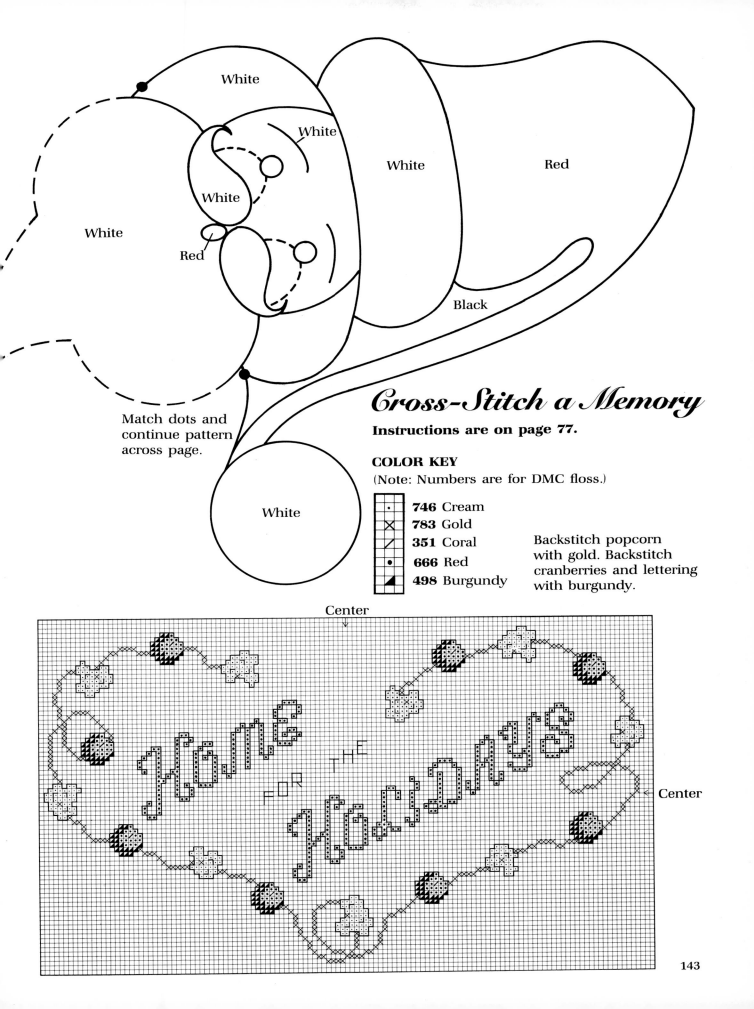

White

White

White

White

Red

White

Black

Red

White

Match dots and
continue pattern
across page.

Cross-Stitch a Memory

Instructions are on page 77.

COLOR KEY
(Note: Numbers are for DMC floss.)

·	**746**	Cream
×	**783**	Gold
⁄	**351**	Coral
•	**666**	Red
◢	**498**	Burgundy

Backstitch popcorn
with gold. Backstitch
cranberries and lettering
with burgundy.

Center

Center

Quilt Two Straight from the Heart

Instructions are on page 70.
Patterns are full-size.
Add ¼″ seam allowance
for all pattern pieces.

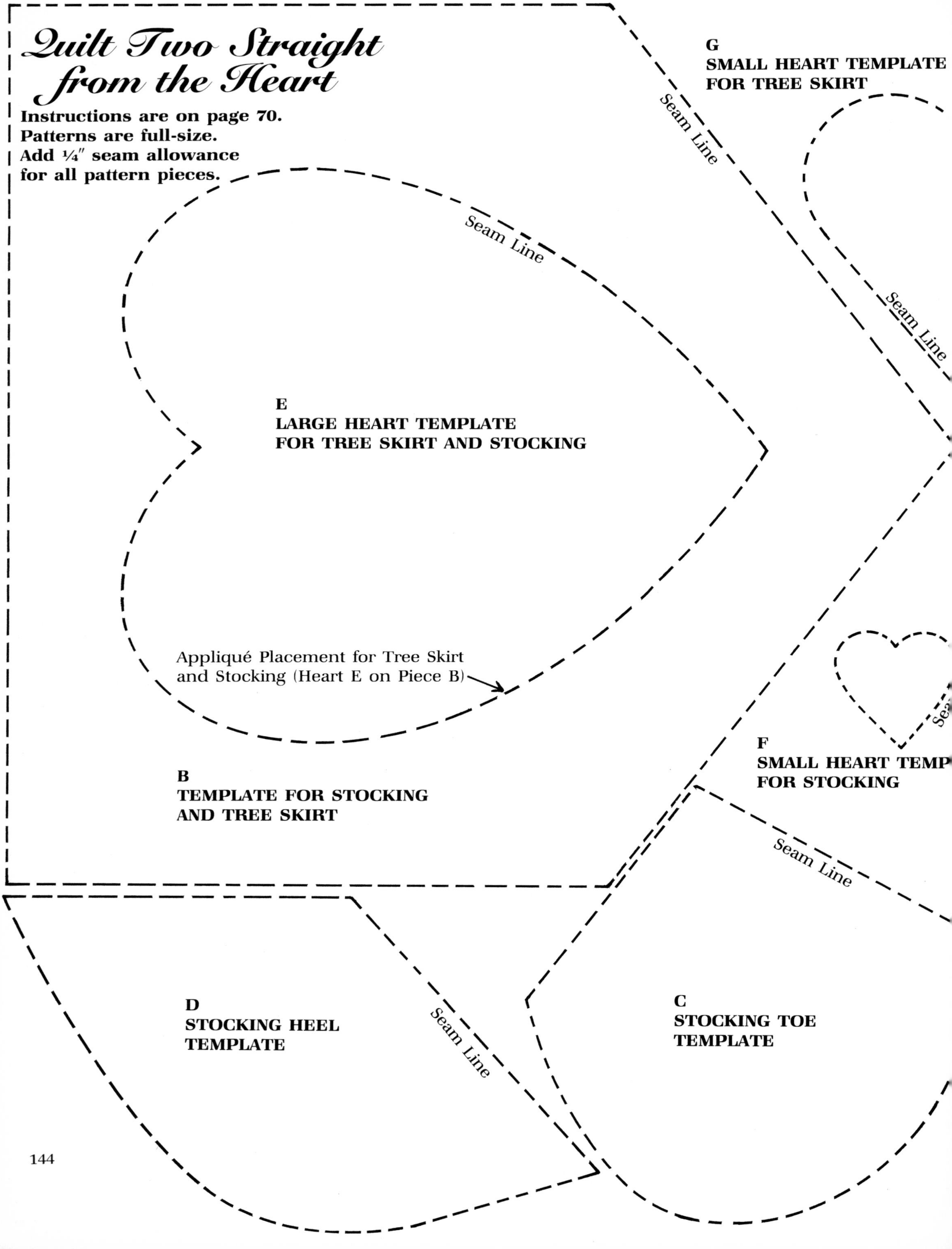

G
SMALL HEART TEMPLATE
FOR TREE SKIRT

Seam Line

Seam Line

Seam Line

E
LARGE HEART TEMPLATE
FOR TREE SKIRT AND STOCKING

Appliqué Placement for Tree Skirt
and Stocking (Heart E on Piece B)

B
TEMPLATE FOR STOCKING
AND TREE SKIRT

F
SMALL HEART TEMP
FOR STOCKING

Seam Line

D
STOCKING HEEL
TEMPLATE

Seam Line

C
STOCKING TOE
TEMPLATE

144

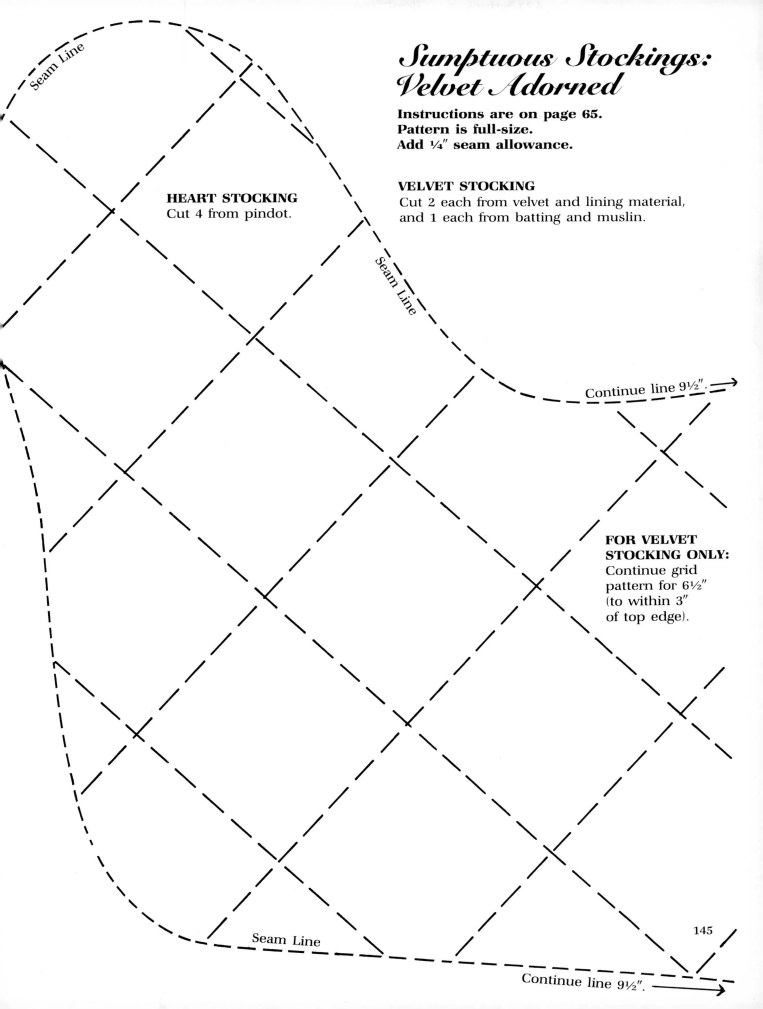

Sumptuous Stockings:
Velvet Adorned

Instructions are on page 65.
Pattern is full-size.
Add ¼″ seam allowance.

VELVET STOCKING

Cut 2 each from velvet and lining material, and 1 each from batting and muslin.

Seam Line

HEART STOCKING
Cut 4 from pindot.

Seam Line

Continue line 9½″. →

FOR VELVET STOCKING ONLY: Continue grid pattern for 6½″ (to within 3″ of top edge).

Seam Line

145

Continue line 9½″. →

Quilt Two Straight from the Heart

(Continued)
Instructions are on page 70.
Patterns are full-size.
Add ¼″ seam allowance
for all pattern pieces.

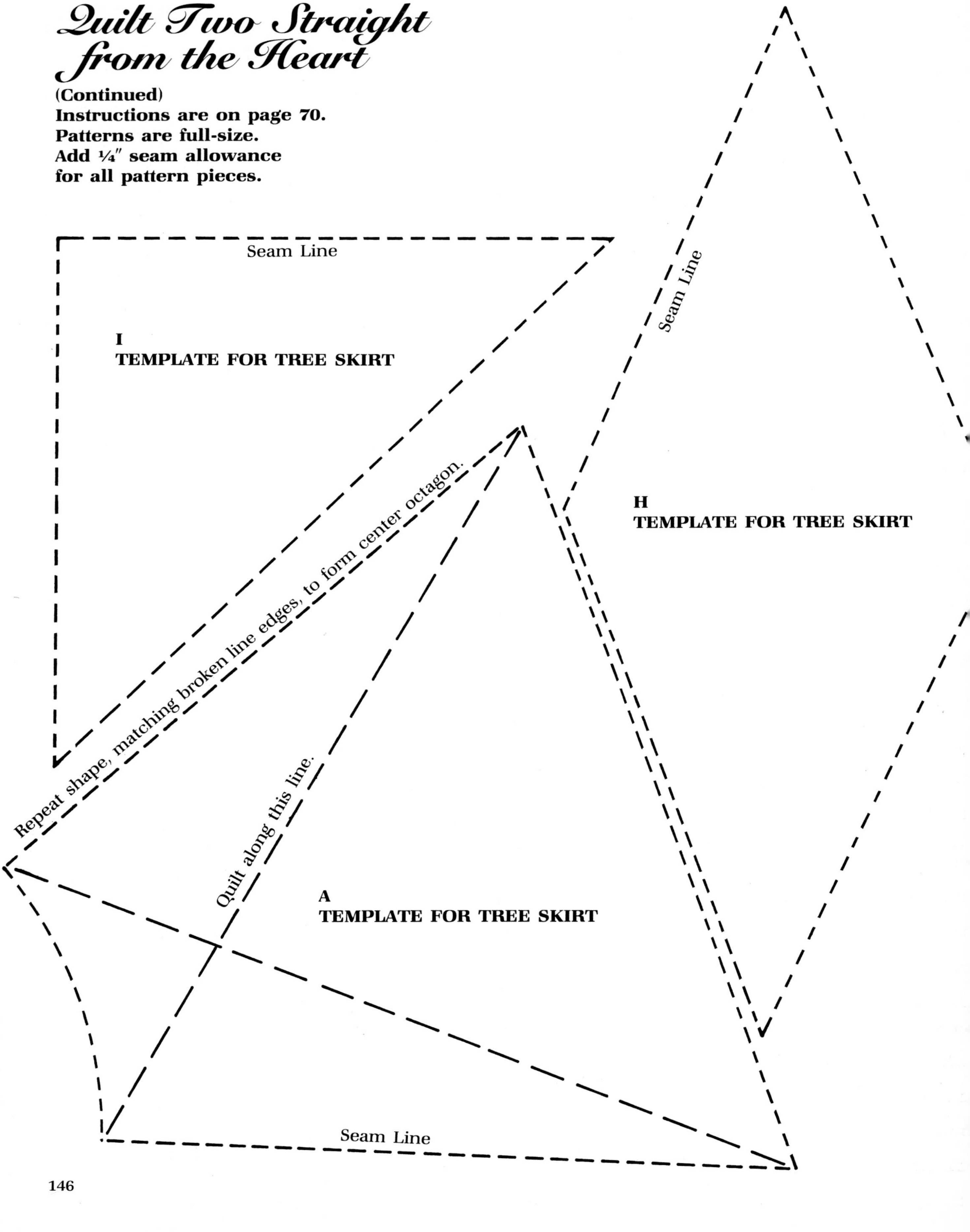

Seam Line

I
TEMPLATE FOR TREE SKIRT

Seam Line

Repeat shape, matching broken line edges, to form center octagon.

H
TEMPLATE FOR TREE SKIRT

Quilt along this line.

A
TEMPLATE FOR TREE SKIRT

Seam Line

Knit a Festive Neighborhood

Instructions are on page 84.

Chart for Knitting

For a 2-story house, add top floor chart to front, and knit another 5 rows to sides and back, adding windows as desired.

Back   Front

Side and Gable   Side and Gable

Top Floor Chart for Front

Sweetly Scented Accessories

Instructions are on page 60.
Patterns are full-size.

BASKET HEART

GARLAND HEART

Poinsettias in Versatile Needlepoint

Instructions are on page 90.

STITCH DIAGRAMS

CONTINENTAL STITCH

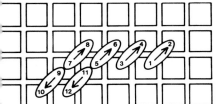

OVERCAST STITCH

SLANTED GOBELIN

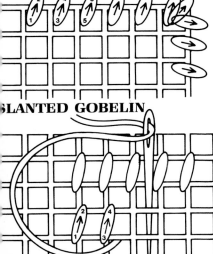

COLOR KEY
(Note: Numbers are for DMC floss.)

/	**666**	Light Red
•	**321**	Medium Red
/	**498**	Dark Red
⊙	**725**	Gold
∂	**909**	Light Green
✕	**890**	Dark Green
	310	Black

Use black in unmarked areas. Use 1 strand of black for backstitching.

FOR BELT BUCKLE, cut out slots for belt before working design.

147

A Sweater with Seasonal Style

**Instructions are
on page 68.**

With gold thread, use duplicate stitch to separate logs, make tree garland, and outline wreath bow.

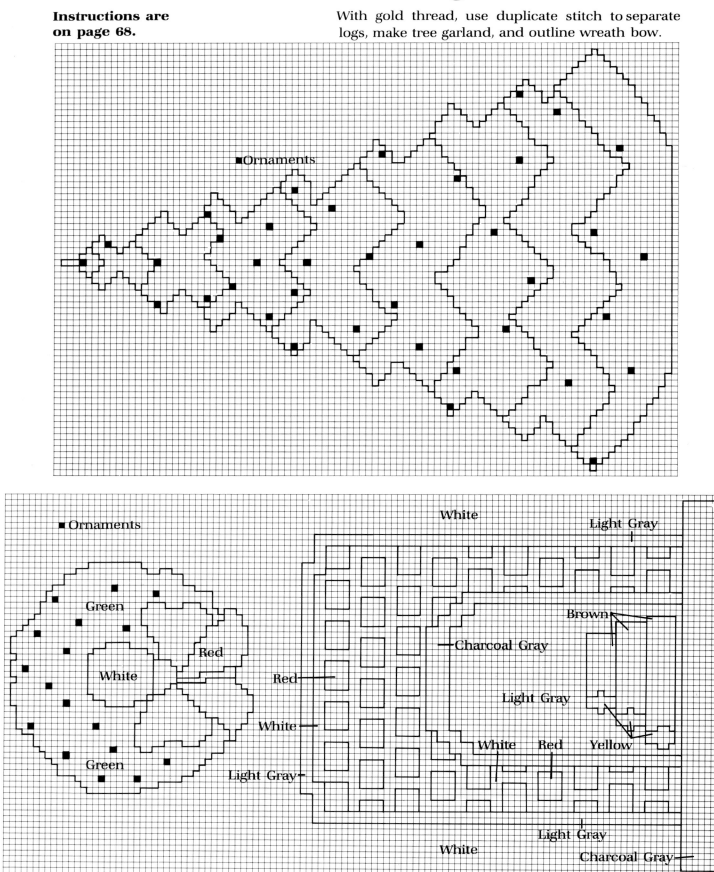

Food Jar Finery

structions are on page 92.

EF'S HAT JAR TOPPER
art for Cross-Stitch

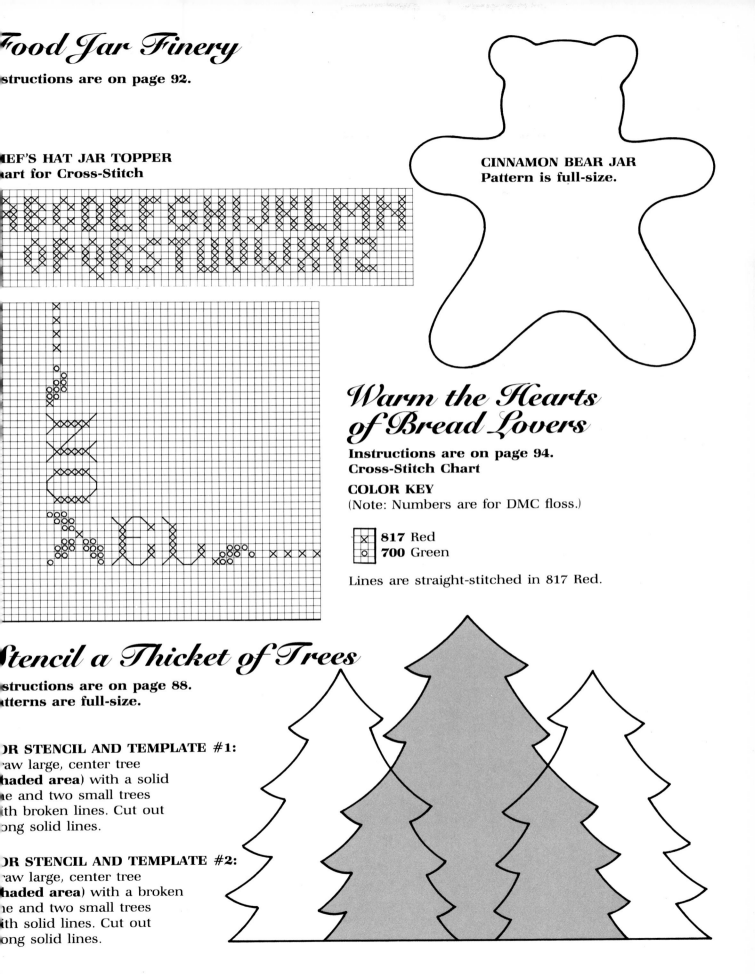

CINNAMON BEAR JAR
Pattern is full-size.

Warm the Hearts of Bread Lovers

Instructions are on page 94.
Cross-Stitch Chart

COLOR KEY
(Note: Numbers are for DMC floss.)

✕	**817** Red
○	**700** Green

Lines are straight-stitched in 817 Red.

Stencil a Thicket of Trees

structions are on page 88.
tterns are full-size.

R STENCIL AND TEMPLATE #1:
aw large, center tree
haded area) with a solid
e and two small trees
th broken lines. Cut out
ong solid lines.

R STENCIL AND TEMPLATE #2:
aw large, center tree
haded area) with a broken
e and two small trees
th solid lines. Cut out
ong solid lines.

These Goodie Bags Are a Cinch

**Instructions are on page 78.
Patterns are full-size.**

**Basket Cover pattern includes ¼"
seam allowance. (Other patterns
are for machine appliqué.)**

"FROM MY KITCHEN" BASKET COVER

FROM MY KITCHEN

HEART
Cut 2 from
red fabric.

COVER
Cut 2 from
red print fabric.

**GINGERBREAD
MAN**
Cut 1 from
brown fabric.

Indentation
for Handle

CENTER CIRCLE
Cut 1 from white fabric
(or 2 if dark fabric
shows through).

"CHRISTMAS BREAD" BAG

CHRISTMAS BREAD

LOAF
Cut 1 from tan fabric.

Placement for Slice

BREAD SLICE
Cut 1 from
white fabric.

LEAF
Cut 5 from
green fabric.

150

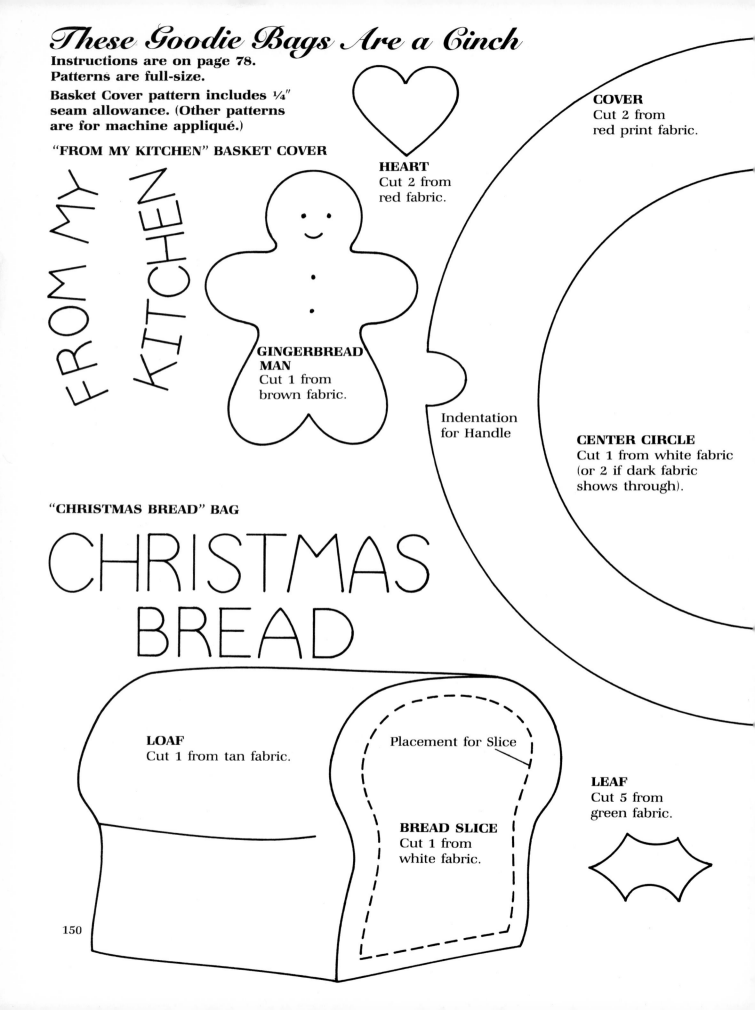

"COOKIES" BAG

STAR COOKIE
Cut 1 from
yellow fabric.

CHOCOLATE COOKIE
Cut 2 from
tan fabric.

Photo Finish:
Holly Leaves
and Berries

Instructions are on page 81.
Pattern is full-size.

COOKIES

Lacy Ornaments from Plain Paper

Instructions are on page 73.
Patterns are full-size.

½ of pattern. Reverse for other half.

½ of pattern. Reverse for other half.

Greetings of Jo

Instructions are on page 76.
Patterns are full-size.

Add ¼″ seam allowance to Front and Back patterns. Oth patterns are for machine appl

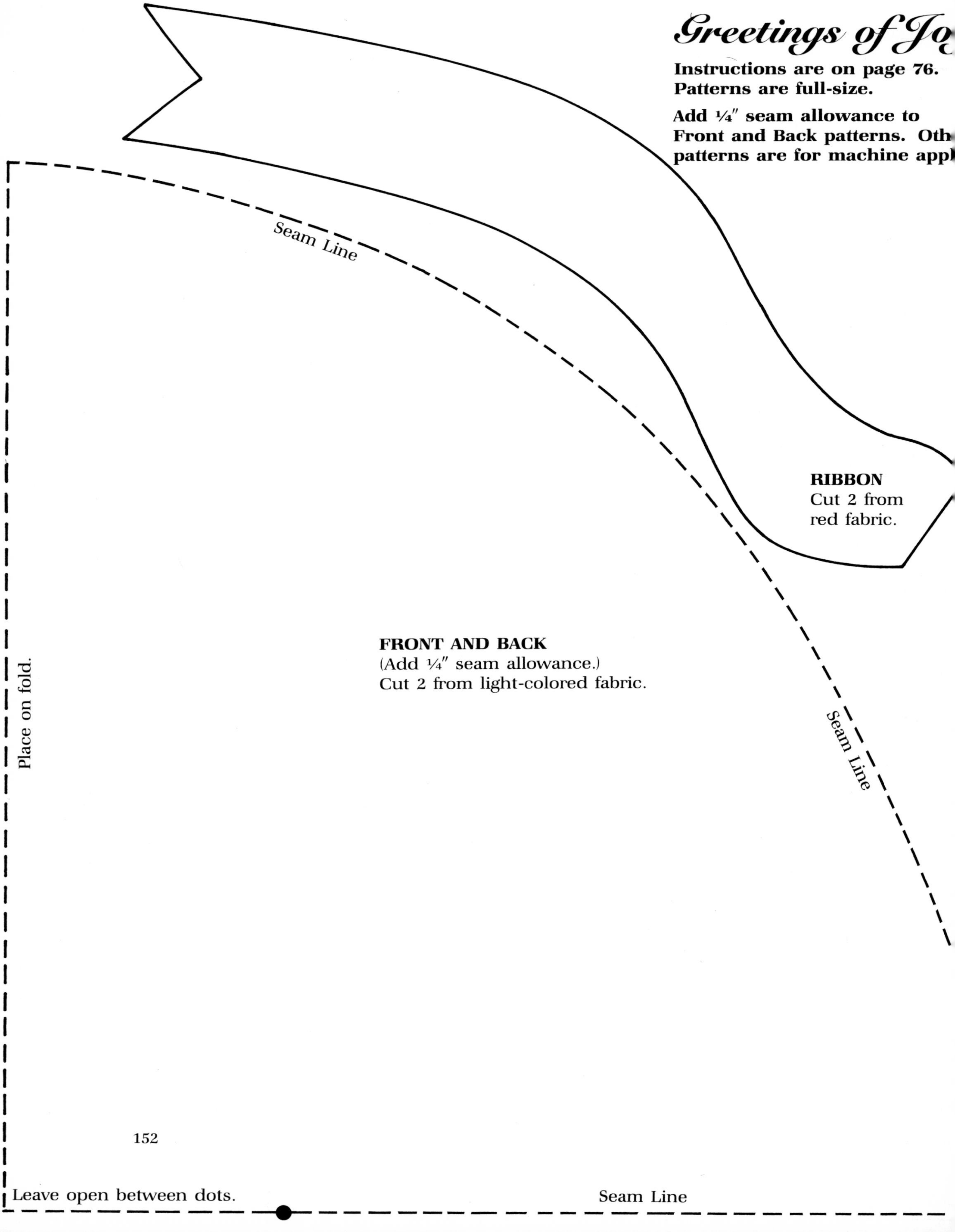

Seam Line
RIBBON
Cut 2 from red fabric.
FRONT AND BACK
(Add ¼″ seam allowance.)
Cut 2 from light-colored fabric.
Seam Line
Place on fold.
Leave open between dots.
Seam Line

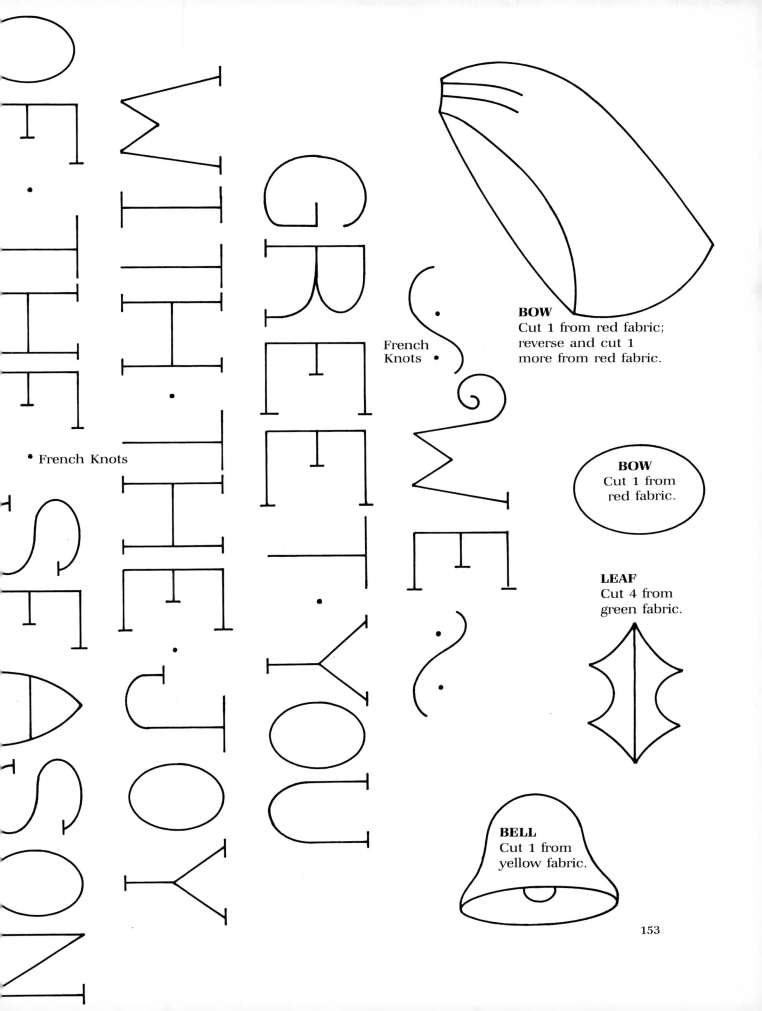

French Knots

• French Knots

BOW
Cut 1 from red fabric;
reverse and cut 1
more from red fabric.

BOW
Cut 1 from
red fabric.

LEAF
Cut 4 from
green fabric.

BELL
Cut 1 from
yellow fabric.

Contributors

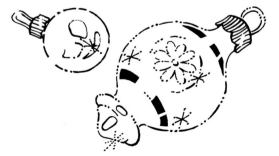

Special thanks to the *Southern Living* Test Kitchens staff for preparing recipes.

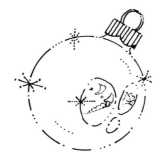

155